To live in the neighbourhood of the Good is fine. If one does not choose to dwell among those who are Good, how will one obtain wisdom?[1]

Bibliographic Information held by the German National Library: The details of the original German edition of this publication are held by the German National Library as part of the German National Bibliography; detailed bibliographical data can be found online at www.dnb.de.

Publisher and Printing:
BoD – Books on Demand, Norderstedt
ISBN 9-783-7534-2312-8

Walther Ziegler

Confucius
in 60 Minutes

Translated by
Alexander Reynolds

My thanks go to Rudolf Aichner for his tireless critical editing; Silke Ruthenberg for the fine graphics; Lydia Pointvogl, Eva Amberger, Christiane Hüttner, and Dr. Martin Engler for their excellent work as manuscript readers and sub-editors; Prof. Guntram Knapp, who first inspired me with enthusiasm for philosophy; and Angela Schumitz, who handled in the most professional manner, as chief editorial reader, the production of both the German and the English editions of this series of books.

My special thanks go to my translator

Dr Alexander Reynolds.

Himself a philosopher, he not only translated the original German text into English with great care and precision but also, in passages where this was required in order to ensure clear understanding, supplemented this text with certain formulations adapted specifically to the needs of English-language readers.

Contents

Confucius's Great Discovery

Confucius (551 – 479 BC) is without doubt the most important of all Chinese philosophers. The name "Confucius" was, in fact, originally an attempt by Latin-speaking Jesuit missionaries, who first translated Confucius's works in 1687, to reproduce the Chinese *Kong Fuzi*, meaning "Master Kong".[2] This latinized form of the name has persisted in the West right up to the present day.

In the years after his death, Confucius's ideas and his doctrine spread first throughout many countries in Asia and later throughout the entire world. Wherever anyone begins a sentence with the words "Confucius says..." the listener is bound to prick up his ears in expectation of hearing some timelessly valid truth about life on which they can model their own behaviour.

And Confucius's thoughts, in fact, remain still today of astonishing contemporary relevance and psychological acuity. Confucius is not just a philosopher but a brilliant psychologist who knows every side of human beings, possessing an unerring eye for our human weaknesses, strengths and potentialities. This perhaps explains how his teachings have been able to survive and persist through two and a half millennia of stormy, convoluted history. Still today, the stamp of Confucius's ideas is plainly visible in the educations, and indeed in the later life-orientations, of billions of human beings not just in China but in Japan, Vietnam, Thailand, Korea, Taiwan and large parts of the Philippines. After the first translations of his works into European languages were made, by Jesuit missionaries, in the course of the 17th century, he began to gain growing attention and respect also in the Western world. The great 18th-century French philosopher, Voltaire, praised him as the first great rationalist and proponent of "Enlightenment". Today, the main work bearing Confucius's name, the famous *Analects*, exists in more than a hundred different translations. The *Analects*, however, are a compilation by the great sage's pupils and disciples. Like Socrates, Confucius himself left us no written works. The Greek-derived word chosen, then, for the standard English translation signifies, appropriately, "selections": short sayings and recounted deeds of the Master assembled into a book after his death. Confucius's "masterpiece", then, is not a systematic work of the sort we know from many of the other great philosophers but rather simply a collection of the views and opinions of Confucius expressed regarding various subjects and themes.[3]

These various dialogues and conversations with pupils contain, however, as Confucius himself insists, a clearly recognizable central idea around which everything turns:

[...] All that I teach can be strung together on a single thread.[4]

What is more, this central idea has something radically new about it. For Confucius, all human beings are, by their very nature, equal. In contradiction to what had been the case in China for thousands of years before him, differences in social class and social origin play no role at all in Confucius's philosophy. Every human being, whether aristocrat or peasant, rich or poor, is capable of finding his "dao", that is to say, the "right way" for him. Every one of us, Confucius teaches, is in principle able, through a process of character-training, education and self-cultivation, to become a "junzi" – or a "gentleman" in Confucius's special sense of this term.

Thanks to these ideas Confucius counts as one of the great thinkers of what has been called the "Axial Age": the age in which, separately but simultaneously on the world's different continents, mankind set off in radically new directions, just as if human thought, after millennia of stasis and "walking on the spot", had suddenly turned on its own axis and passed from darkness out into light.

Thus, Confucius's lifetime coincides almost exactly with that of the Buddha on the Indian sub-continent and that of the Greek philosopher Socrates in distant Europe. Moreover, just like these two other thinkers he gives to humanity, in a period of moral decline and of wars, an entirely new political and ethical orientation, the effects of which have stretched far beyond his lifetime. Like the Buddha and Socrates, Confucius went in search of a timeless truth which would be valid even for future generations. It is not enough, he says, simply to understand one's own time:

A person without concern for what is far away is sure to encounter worries close at hand.[5]

If Confucius's ideas have enjoyed such wide resonance, this is surely owed to his simple but brilliant core idea: the search for the "dao", which is also a search for a threefold harmony: harmony between the individual and his family; harmony between oneself and society; and inner harmony between oneself and one's principles, that is to say, between our real life and our ideal image.

What Confucius was aiming at here was not, however, as one might at first glance assume, the achievement of a total conformity of the individual to his family, his social environment or the state. Nor does he aim at the eventual achievement of a total equality between all individuals or a perfect coincidence between our lives and our ideal images of how human life should be. On the contrary, the striving for harmony means, for Confucius, something fundamentally distinct from the striving to conform or agree:

The gentleman harmonizes and does not merely agree.[6]

"Harmony" in Confucius is a rich and shifting concept that is difficult to grasp. But it is only once we have grasped it that we become really able to understand the key idea behind his philosophy. When he speaks of "harmony" Confucius is not using the term in its colloquial sense and referring to a relaxed state without tensions. On the contrary, he is referring to a tireless, lifelong striving. "Harmony", for him, is nothing other than a persistent striving for a co-humanity that would be worthy of its name. When Confucius was asked by one of his pupils whether there was "one word that could serve as a guide for one's entire life", he replied:

Is it not "understanding"?[7]

Going on to elucidate the Chinese word "shu" that is rendered here as "understanding", he reveals that it is in fact a matter of that basic moral principle, recurring in so many forms in so many cultures, which is called "the golden rule"[8] and which runs:

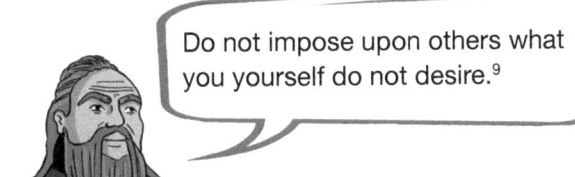

Do not impose upon others what you yourself do not desire.[9]

But just this "understanding", construed in just this sense, is far from being something obvious and self-evident. On the contrary. Putting oneself in a position such that one feels what others feel is the hardest thing in the world. Not a single one of us, Confucius argues, ever really succeeds in taking the needs of others into account in just the way we take our own. Normally, we place our own interests high above the wellbeing of others, so that injuries to this wellbeing often occur in daily life.

It is only the "junzi", the true "gentleman" in Confucius's sense, who succeeds in living his own life without impairing the lives of others. This "gentleman", indeed, even consciously promotes the development of the other people around him. In principle, Confucius believes, any human being can rise, through training of his character and self-cultivation, to become such a "gentleman". He concedes, however, that it is an extremely difficult thing to feel, think and act, in every situation, as a "junzi". He himself, he admits, has not always been up to the task, since it demands the exercise of three virtues at the same time:

> The way of the gentleman is threefold and yet I have not been able to achieve any aspect of it. The good do not worry; the wise are not confused; and the courageous do not fear.[10]

Confucius surely deserves respect for admitting that even he, the great philosopher and teacher, "had not yet been able to achieve" all three aspects of this threefold virtue, that is, to be at once understanding, wise and courageous. The key moral appeal that he makes, however, is the appeal never to leave off trying to be all these things. The great task, argues Confucius, is that of bringing the two forces of egoism and understanding for others, which so easily drift apart from one another, into harmony. Because it is only if we succeed in doing this that we have a chance of a fulfilled life. True happiness, Confucius argues, requires the development of "ren", or "humanity":

When it comes to humanity, defer to no one, not even your teacher.[11]

This key philosophical idea, the resolute search for harmony via understanding and humanity, may on first consideration appear to be something bland and obvious. But considered more closely, what Confucius has seized on here is an extremely vital and controversial topic. Harmony is in fact nothing that can be considered self-evident. On the contrary, it is always the exception. We all know how conflictual family relationships can be; we have all become enraged about the state, our own powerlessness in the face of it, and the whims of bureaucratic authorities; and we all know the painful feeling of failing to realize one's own wishes and potentialities. How, though, are we to deal with our own dissatisfaction? Is it possible for us ever to attain the "threefold harmony"?

Confucius expresses the eternal fundamental conflict of human existence which each of us knows only too well from his or her own life: we are all born with needs, wishes and drives; but we are not alone in the world; our needs and wishes tend to clash with those of other human beings and cannot always be brought to reconciliation with them.

There is competition and struggle over scarce goods, attention, fame, recognition, affection and love. Feelings of envy, vanity or deeply-felt personal injury are as old as mankind itself. Confucius was the first to dare to throw some light on this field of tensions and to pose the all-decisive question: how can I develop myself, and bring my own wishes and ideas to realization, without thereby limiting or harming others? How can I follow the laws and customs of my community and my state without thereby denying my own self? In which situations must I insist on the expression and development of my own values and in which must I draw back and let other values prevail? When must I faithfully support my friends, family and government and when I must speak out against them and resist them?

It is precisely because Confucius poses questions which affect us all in our daily lives that his teachings are so helpful and practical. The practical applicability and psychological acuity of his ideas are also perhaps due to his own personal history and experiences. Confucius knew life both from the perspective of the poor man without resources and from that of the rich and powerful. He lost his father already at the age of three and saw his family sink into poverty. Almost an orphan, he grew up in very straitened circumstances:

In my youth I was of humble status, so I became proficient in many humble tasks.[12]

Confucius worked early on as a cowherd and even in his later life knew periods of great privation and poverty. He succeeded, indeed, already at the age of twenty-two in founding a school of his own which had soon acquired more than three thousand pupils and even rose for a time, if the tradition is to be believed,[13] to the high rank of an administrator bearing the title of minister. He was, however, if we are to continue to trust the tradition, very soon removed from this position by political disruptions. He then, we are told, lived as an itinerant teacher, moving from place to place with his students, for some fourteen years before returning to his home town and continuing to teach there until the end of his life.

Of what use could this ancient wisdom of Confucius possibly be to us today? Was he right in holding the search for the "dao", the "right way", through the re-alization of outer and inner harmony to be the most important thing in any human life? And if so, how are we to find this harmony? Does the highest happi-ness consist in fitting smoothly into the family and in showing an empathetic understanding of others? Or does the individual, by striving for this, fall into the trap of conformity? What precisely does Confucius mean by his demand that we resolutely and uncom-promisingly bring into being "ren", or true human-ity? Confucius has been giving extremely concrete answers to these questions – and this already for the last two and a half thousand years.

Confucius's Central Idea

The Secret of Harmony: "Xiao" and "Li" – Respect, Rites and Rituals

Harmony is, for Confucius, not just an ideal that we should strive for but above all a way of living our lives which we can apply and bring to full realization. There are, he argues, two roots, or two ancient models of behaviour, which can contribute to bringing harmony into our daily lives. These are "xiao" and "li". We often apply these two things so naturally and unquestioningly that we are not even aware of the subtle, implicit effect that they are having.

"Xiao" means "respect for one another" and also, sometimes, "piety" or "sense of duty". "Li" is the Chinese word for rites, rituals, customs, laws, rules, agreements and traditions. These two terms "xiao" and "li" are key concepts in Confucius's philosophy. The meaning of "xiao" is, at bottom, a very simple one. It signifies respect for one's parents and, by association with this, respect for one's superior in one's profession, one's government or one's state.

The original meaning of the word, however, remains recognizable in its written character:

This character consists of the sign for "age", also meaning "old" or "parents"

combined with the sign for "child".

The combination, however, is one, significantly, in which "old" is placed above "child". The idea, then, is conveyed already by the very pictogram for "respect" that respect is something that places parents, and older people in general, above younger people and children, urging that the former should be revered and cared for by the latter. Care and reverence for parents, however, should not, argues Confucius, be misunderstood to mean simply seeing to it that one's parents' physical needs continue to be seen to once their ability to earn their own living has declined:

[...] Even dogs and horses are provided with nourishment. If you are not respectful (to one's parents) wherein lies the difference?[14]

"Xiao", then, signifies much more than just seeing to someone's physical needs. The notion comprises not only, for example, the child's showing love to the parent and his presence at the latter's deathbed, but also the revering of still older ancestors and obedience not only to the parents themselves but also to older siblings and to those placed above one in one's profession. Each person must take on his role in a spirit of respect with regard to others:

Let the lord be a true lord, the ministers true ministers, the fathers true fathers and the sons true sons.[15]

Confucius warns against seeking conflict too easily and being too ready to put into question, by revolutions, revolts and uprisings, a hierarchy which has grown up organically over many years. He recommends that we remain, rather, moderate and circumspect:

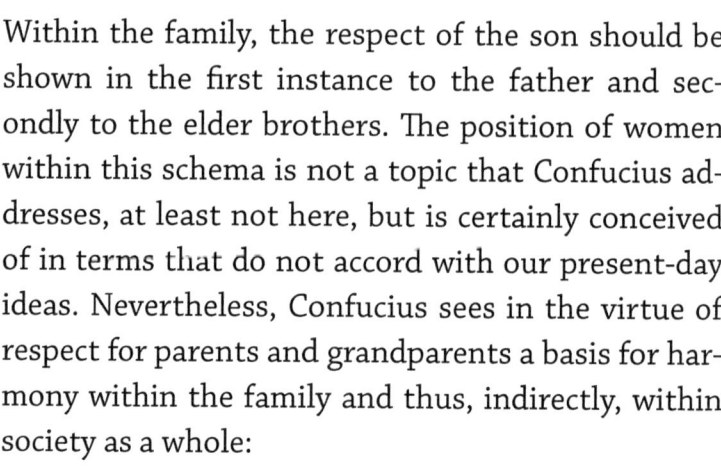

Acquiring virtue by applying the mean – is that not the best? And yet among the common people few are able to practice this virtue for long.[16]

Within the family, the respect of the son should be shown in the first instance to the father and secondly to the elder brothers. The position of women within this schema is not a topic that Confucius addresses, at least not here, but is certainly conceived of in terms that do not accord with our present-day ideas. Nevertheless, Confucius sees in the virtue of respect for parents and grandparents a basis for harmony within the family and thus, indirectly, within society as a whole:

[...] In being a filial son and good brother one is already taking part in government. What need is there, then, to speak of "participating in government"?[17]

With his use of the key term "li" Confucius is alluding to those customs, rules, rites and rituals which had grown up organically throughout hundreds of years of Chinese history. These change, indeed, over time but provide a means of orientation precisely because they are the products of such a long process of formation and have become finer and more subtle over the years. On being asked by one of his pupils whether it was possible for their generation to know what sort of rites and rituals would be observed ten generations on from then, Confucius replied:

The Yin followed the rituals of the Xia, altering them only in ways that we know. The Zhou followed the rituals of the Yin, altering them only in ways that we know. If some dynasty succeeds the Zhou, we can know what it will be like even a hundred generations from now.[18]

One can confidently expect, then, that each generation, while making ever finer and better the rites and rituals that they inherit, will nevertheless continue to build on the rites and rituals of those who came before. In Confucius's day there were no written laws or law-books, so that observing certain principles of law and certain customs and usages that had been handed down was an eminently important matter. The "li" form an important means of orientation for people in their everyday lives, inasmuch as they comprise rites and rituals, great and small, that serve to harmonize our co-existence with one another. Confucius uses the example of archery to illustrate this. His pupils did, in fact, learn such skills as archery and charioteering besides the more usual academic subjects such as writing, arithmetic, literature and traditional rites and music. Aiming and striking with the bow, Confucius believed, promoted the powers of concentration and self-discipline. But it also, and above all, served to promote mutual recognition and respect. Just as, today, boxers bump their boxing gloves before a fight or karate fighters bow to one another, so too did Confucius's pupils bow to one another before a contest. The winner of the contest also always poured the defeated party a cup of wine:

> Before mounting the stairs to the archery hall gentlemen bow and defer to one another and after descending from the hall they mutually offer up toasts.[19]

Confucius placed great value on such rituals because he recognized how important they were for harmony among human beings. No matter how much competitiveness and rivalry there may be in sport, in daily life, in the family or in society, these gestures of mutual respect and recognition create at least a moment, even if no more than a moment, in which we recall to mind our shared humanity. The same applies to such rites as funerals, which are ritualized participations in collective mourning by those who survive a loved one, to the solemn inaugurations of monarchs, presidents and other rulers, to feasts and holidays which have their own rites and rituals, and even to the simple everyday rituals consisting in forms of greeting. Even today the shaking of hands, the singing of anthems and the exchanging of pennants form part of all international sporting events, such as football World Cups and other such competitions. Confucius understands why this is so important:

Find inspiration in the Odes. Take your place through ritual [...][20]

Although we barely notice it, people all over the world use what might be called "ritual actions" to greet one another, regardless of whether they are old or new acquaintances. In Asia this mostly takes the form of bows, in Europe or America the form of handshakes. The French kiss on the cheek. Indians have a more complex ritual: they greet each other with the word "namaste", meaning "I bow before you", while the palms of the hands are pressed together and raised to the height of the chest, the head being slightly lowered as this is done.

Through performing these simple gestures we inform the person we are greeting that he can feel safe and secure and that we will deal with him in a polite, respectful and trusting way within the framework of certain fixed forms of interaction. This is why Confucius placed great value on "xiao" and "li", or on the respectful search for harmony in family and society and in the observance, to this end, of customs and rituals. What mattered to him above all was the maintenance of a functioning community in which the outer form supported the inward connection and cohesion. On the other hand, however, rituals and traditional rules were not, for Confucius, ends in themselves. They needed to be authentic:

> When it comes to mourning, it is better to be excessively sorrowful than fastidious.[21]

When he was asked by a pupil whether it would not be better to deliberately exceed the prescribed measure of conformity to ethical behaviour, so as to be absolutely sure of not accidentally falling short of it, Confucius replied:

Overshooting the mark is just as bad as falling short of it.[22]

But the observance of "xiao" and "li", respect and ritual, is limited, in Confucius's thought, also by a second factor: the specifically human failing that consists in recognizing duties but not having the strength to perform them. Confucius seems even to accuse himself of this failing:

Abroad, to serve the high ministers and officers; at home, to serve one's father and elder brother; in all duties to the dead, not to dare not to exert oneself; and not to be overcome of wine – what one of these things do I attain to?[23]

We might note here two especially interesting details. Firstly, that Confucius speaks almost in the same breath of the effort made "not to be overcome of wine" and of the effort to observe the duties of family piety and to fulfil all obligations both vis-à-vis the living and vis-à-vis the dead. Secondly, that he regretfully acknowledges that he has perhaps attained to none of these goals himself. We do in fact find Confucius expressing a certain humorous scepticism about his own complete moral maturity at several points in the *Analects* besides this one. Clearly, Confucius wants to convey to us the idea that no one is really able, in the last analysis, to comport himself as a flawless moral model for all:

I have yet to meet someone who is able to perceive his own faults and then take himself to task inwardly.[24]

In order to discover the "threefold harmony", i.e. harmony with family and friends, harmony with society, and harmony with one's own life, what is first needed is an education taking the character to higher levels and an opening-up of the character. We need to free ourselves of our petty egoism and our selfishness and become a "junzi", or a "gentleman" in the fullest sense. "Junzi", indeed, is an absolutely central concept in Confucius's ethics.

Exemplary Thinking and Acting: The Five Virtues of the "Junzi", or the True "Gentleman"

A "junzi" is a kind of knightly figure: a noble individual with fully developed virtues or, in modern terms, a fair and responsible citizen and human being. Ultimately, Confucius's vision was one of creating an ideal society consisting entirely of such "junzi"s, who would acknowledge one another as such, each seeing to the self-development of the others.

At the time when Confucius took it up "junzi" was still a word used solely for born aristocrats and princes of actual noble blood. The Chinese character for "junzi" consists of the sign for "lord" combined with the sign for "son". That is to say, it conveys the meaning: "son of the lord", "son of the ruler" or "son of the prince", expressing the idea of great power or status conferred by birth alone. Confucius, however, took this concept and completely re-defined it in terms of his own new system of thought. In Confucius's work, "junzi" is no longer someone of noble birth but much rather someone who, regardless of his birth, proves to be of noble character. There is clearly something

radically modern in this innovation. If it is no longer social origin, or "good blood", that is the decisive
factor, but rather nobility of character, then any one
of us can, in principle, become a "true gentleman",
regardless of whether we are born in a slum or on
one of the grand boulevards, of whether our parents are rich and cultured or poor and near-illiterate.
Each one of us is capable forming and developing his
character. The starting point is the same for us all.
Because, argues Confucius, we all have very similar
basic natural predispositions:

By nature, people are similar;
they diverge as the result of
practice.[25]

In essence, then, we are all the same and it is education that is the decisive factor. This means that even
someone born very poor can rise to become a "noble
man", just as a prince or the son of a prince can be or
become morally ignoble. If this occurs, says Confucius, he can no longer count as a "junzi":

If the gentleman abandons Goodness, how can he merit the name?[26]

A truly "noble" person, then, is measured not by his blood or social origin but rather solely by his thoughts and actions:

If a gentleman is not serious, he will not inspire awe [...].[27]

But what is it exactly that distinguishes the "junzi"? How is he different from others? In the first place, Confucius tells of a whole series of specific styles of behaviour:

The gentleman is not motivated by the desire for a full belly or a comfortable abode. He is simply scrupulous in behaviour and simple in speech, drawing near to those who possess the Way in order to be set straight by them. Surely this and nothing else is what it means to love learning.[28]

This, then, is Confucius's revolutionary new contention: the virtues that characterize the true gentleman are not innate but can be learned. Although Confucius lived in what was still very much a class-divided, feudally stratified society, he himself made no distinction between classes and taught pupils from all social strata. His teaching consisted essentially in teaching them the five cardinal virtues and how to practice them:

Reverence, magnanimity, trustworthiness, diligence and kindness. If you are reverent, you will avoid disgrace; if you are

> magnanimous, you will win the populace; if you are trustworthy, others will put their trust in you; if you are diligent, you will achieve results; and if you are kind, you will have the wherewithal to employ the people.[29]

The first of these virtues, reverence, consists in showing respect to others. An important role is played here by the concepts we have examined above: "xiao" and "li", rituals and forms of human interaction. In all one's contacts with others, from the polite form of greeting right through to friendly ways of taking leave, these forms and rituals show to the other person that one is making an effort to come to an understanding with him or her in a trusting, humane way within practices of social inter-relation that have grown up organically and proven themselves over time. These forms show, in other words, that interaction will go on, if it goes on at all, within the framework of codes of behaviour which assure both parties that their human dignity will be acknowledged.

The second virtue that needs to be learned if one is to become a true gentleman is magnanimity. Learning this virtue is a matter of getting one's own vanity under control and of encouraging the self-development of others. It is especially important not to condemn people even if one feels that they are misunderstanding you or remaining unresponsive to you:

To be patient even when others do not understand – is this not the mark of the gentleman?[30]

To keep one's patience even when understanding and acknowledgment are refused one is indeed a noble quality. Most people would react with annoyance or take offence. Essential to the virtue of magnanimity, then, is the overcoming of one's own vanity. This is so, moreover, not just in the case of insults perceived to have been received from others but also in the case of mistakes one has made oneself. When we have done something wrong, we tend not to want to admit it, to cover it up, or to stubbornly defend our position even after we have realized it is wrong. It is very rare that someone frankly admits that they were in error and draws all the conclusions that follow from this error. But the true gentleman must be able to do just this:

If you have committed a transgression, do not be afraid to change your ways.[31]

When a man is rebuked with exemplary words after having made a mistake [...] what is important is that he change himself in order to accord with them.[32]

The third cardinal virtue is trustworthiness. By this is meant, above all, that the true gentleman brings his deeds into harmony with his words. He does not lie and does not promise what he cannot perform:

The gentleman is ashamed to have his words exceed his actions.[33]

The gentleman is displeased when someone fails to express his true intentions but rather thinks up pretexts for his actions.[34]

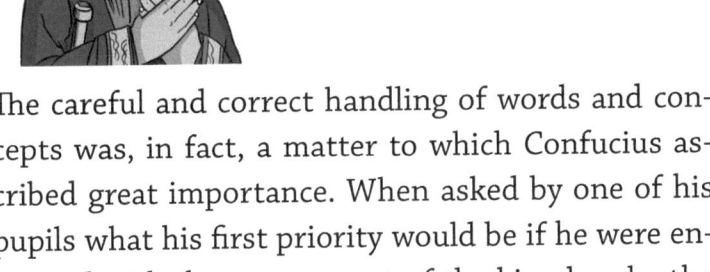

The careful and correct handling of words and concepts was, in fact, a matter to which Confucius ascribed great importance. When asked by one of his pupils what his first priority would be if he were entrusted with the government of the kingdom by the ruler of the state of Wei, Confucius replied:

It would, of course, be the rectification of names.[35]

Confucius was a great critic of the sloppy and inaccurate practices that had spread in China during this period with regard to the use of names and concepts. For example, the round pots and vases which had come into use by this time were still, he noted with disapproval, being designated by the same term as had been used to designate the square pots and vases that had been used in earlier epochs. Confucius's primary concern, however, was the "rectification" of terms and concepts that were being used for political purposes. The pupil who had posed the question retorted, the *Analects* tell us, to his master's answer with the words: "Can you, Master, really be so far off the mark? Why worry about rectifying names?" This provoked Confucius to further elucidate his view, saying:

If names are not rectified, speech will not accord with reality; when speech does not accord with reality, things will not be successfully accomplished; when things are not

successfully accomplished, ritual practice and music will fail to flourish; [...] then the common people will be at a loss as to what to do with themselves. This is why the gentleman only applies names that can be properly spoken [...].[36]

The fourth cardinal virtue is diligence. The mention of this quality may at first seem odd; but Confucius considers that the ceaseless diligent effort to develop oneself to higher and higher levels is a very important precondition for all character-formation. Each one of us, indeed, has the basic natural equipment for rising to become a "true gentleman". But we must want to do so:

> I will not open the door for a mind that is not already striving to understand, nor will I provide words for a tongue that is not already struggling to speak.[37]

The fifth and most important virtue that the "true gentleman" must develop is kindness. This term, in Confucius, does not bear just the usual, colloquial sense of "being kind" to people in the sense of doing them little favours and so on; it also connotes a much broader, higher sense of participation in a shared co-humanity, or what Classical Chinese calls "ren":

> Whoever intervenes unerringly in favour of the Good, urges constantly toward what is right, and desires concord and harmony – such a man can be called educated.[38]

To "intervene in favour of the Good" also means: not to place the achievement of one's own wishes and goals, nor even the development of one's own personality, above the wishes, goals and development of others. The "junzi" constantly has the good of others in mind and must, for this reason, always behave exemplarily, so as to inspire enthusiasm for such behaviour also in other people:

> If you cannot correct yourself, how can you expect to correct others?[39]

The "junzi" must, quite generally, be a model to others in both his thinking and his behaviour. Indeed, he must apply still stricter standards to himself than he does to those around him:

The gentleman seeks it in himself. The petty person seeks it in others.[40]

At one point during his years as an itinerant teacher, namely the year 489 BC, Confucius and his pupils found themselves in a region that had been laid waste by war and ran very short of food and supplies. When the pupils felt barely able to go on from lack of nourishment, they asked Confucius what they should do. He replied:

Of course, the gentleman (too) encounters hardship. The difference is that the petty man, encountering hardship, is overwhelmed by it.[41]

To sum up, then: there have, of course, been descriptions also in other countries and cultures than the Chinese of the sort of sets of "cardinal virtues" that make up, in Confucius, the character of the "true gentleman". The samurai in Japan or the knight of medieval European history and legend are very similar ideal models for how to live one's life "nobly". The deeds of such knights and samurai are described in epics and fairy tales that those born in these cultures learn by heart from early childhood on. The especially provocative element in Confucius's ethics, however, consists in the fact that the virtues of Confucius's "true gentleman" are virtues that *can be learned* or, in other words, virtues that no longer have any connection with "noble blood" or "high social origin".

For this reason, one absolutely decisive building-block in Confucius's philosophy is the notion of the individual's self-cultivation and self-perfection through education.

"In Education There Are No Differences in Kind". Everything Presupposes Education But Education is Not Everything.

That education plays an outstandingly important role in Confucius's thought is clear right from the *Analects'* opening "excerpt" from the Master's sayings:

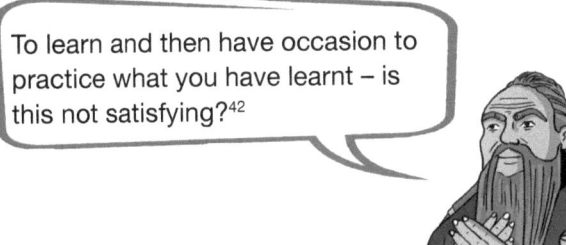

To learn and then have occasion to practice what you have learnt – is this not satisfying?[42]

But more important still, perhaps, is his unmistakable, uncompromising demand that there be free access to education for all:

In education, there are no distinctions concerning who is taught.[43]

Even two and a half millennia later, we are still working on bringing to realization this Confucian ideal. Because tuition fees remain a feature of the education systems in many societies around the world. It also remains the case that a disproportionate number of students come from upper- and middle-class backgrounds. Confucius's demand for free and equal access to education is all the more impressive because in his China of around 500 BC it really was only the richest and most powerful members of the population who had any chance of learning to read or write at all. Confucius, however, made a point of seeing to it that, in his school, even pupils from the lowest and simplest strata of society could pursue courses of study. They were allowed to do so even if they could pay little, or almost nothing at all:

> I have never denied instruction to anyone who, of their own accord, offered up as little as a bundle of silk or bit of cured meat.[44]

He educated his pupils so as to make of them "true gentlemen" and trained them to perform duties as civil servants and administrators. Some, indeed, did go on to take on high political offices. The number of these latter was, of course, limited, since most ministerial and administrative posts were still assigned on the basis of "good family", not on that of success in learning and education. Confucius disapproved of these practices and recommended another course entirely:

Those of my disciples who were first to enter into study [...] with me were simple rustics, whereas those who entered later were aristocrats. If I had to employ them [in public office] I would prefer the first.[45]

One should not, of course, envisage the school of Confucius as if it were a present-day university. The primary purpose of the school was to acquaint the pupils with various texts handed down by ancient tradition: texts bearing on law and order in the form of the *Book of Documents*, texts bearing on poetry and culture in the form of the *Book of Odes*, and texts bearing on history and custom in the form of the *Book of Rites*. In addition, certain practical skills were taught and learnt, such as archery and charioteering. In a broad and general sense, however, the goal pursued by the education offered at the school was that of a schooling of the character, a kind of set of instructions for self-cultivation. The cultivation of the character, particularly its cultivation to points of real refinement, is a process that is never concluded: a lifelong task from the cradle to the grave. No one, so argues Confucius, comes naturally, with fully developed knowledge and nobility, into the world. Were such a case to occur, although Confucius viewed such a thing as near-impossible, this would indeed be an instance of the very highest level of knowledge:

> Those who are born understanding it are the best; those who come to understand it through learning are second; those who find it difficult to understand and yet persist in their studies come next; people who find it difficult to understand but do not even try to learn are the worst of all.[46]

Regarding his own self, Confucius says:

I am not someone who was born with knowledge.[47]

In order to improve and increase one's knowledge, Confucius goes on, what is necessary is not only the study of books but also the living exchange of thoughts with other human beings. For this reason, it is always worth one's while to listen to other people and not to insist stubbornly on one's own personal view:

When walking with two other people, I will always find a teacher among them. I focus on those who are good and seek to emulate them [...].[48]

If Confucius frequently emphasizes that even he sometimes learned things from other people, we should not interpret this as false modesty or coquettishness. The idea, revived today, of "lifelong learning" is one, in fact, that had already been expressed by Confucius. We need, he argued, to remain open, our whole life long, to the new and to think over critically whatever it is we learn, supplementing it or replacing it where necessary:

> Both keeping past teachings alive and understanding the present – someone able to do this is worthy of being a teacher.[49]

It is important both to think carefully about what one has learned while, at the same time, checking the thoughts that one has by comparing them both with the knowledge one already possesses and with the experience one has acquired:

> If you learn without thinking about what you have learned, you will be lost. If you think without learning, however, you will fall into danger.[50]

Someone, for example, who merely follows his own thoughts and meditations before he has studied sufficiently or acquired sufficient experience will tend to try to subjugate reality too radically and completely to his own ideas and notions:

Loving uprightness without balancing it with a love for learning will result in the vice of intolerance.[51]

On the other hand, it is useless to engage in intensive study and pile up a great deal of knowledge without ever personally, critically thinking through what one has learned. Why is this so? Confucius illustrates the point with an example:

Imagine a person who can recite the several hundred odes by heart but, when delegated a government task, is unable to carry it out [...] No

matter how many odes he might have memorized, what good are they to him?[52]

It is essential, then, to any true education that that which has been learned be also correctly applied. Necessary, in other words, is a certain moral or ethical orientation:

> Whoever intervenes unerringly in favour of the Good, urges constantly toward what is right, and desires concord and harmony – such a man can be called educated.[53]

But how can we recognize "the Good"? Here, a decisive step forward is made in Confucius's philosophical thinking. Although the first "movement", as it were, of this philosophy consists in the assigning of great value to a lifelong process of learning and education, its "second movement" consists in an argument that, although education is very important, it is not absolutely everything. If one wishes to apply what one has learned, one needs an additional criterion by which one can judge and adjust one's actions and one's general conduct in life. This criterion is what Confucius calls "ren", or true humanity.

Bringing "Ren", or "True Humanity", into Being

The Chinese word "ren", which means "humanity" in the strong moral sense of the term, is the most important, and most often used, of the concepts deployed in Confucius's texts. In the *Analects* alone it occurs more than a hundred times. One may say, then, that if one has understood the notion of "ren" one has understood Confucius's core idea. This idea exceeds in importance all the others. Respect, or "xiao", and the observance of the rites, or "li", are important, indeed. The "junzi"'s cultivation of the virtues even more so. The decisive thing, however, and the crowning of the whole construction, is "ren". In the last analysis, it is only the person who practices "ren" who acts justly and correctly. It is only "ren" that provides the "junzi" with the standard or criterion which enables him to apply his virtues and his education in the service of the right ends.

But what does "ren" mean? What, concretely, does Confucius understand by "humanity"? We can find an initial indication of this already in the Chinese character itself. The character "ren" consists, in its left-hand half, of the pictogram for "human being", showing a person walking or standing:

and in its right-hand half of the signs for the number "two", which is written in Chinese not, as it is in Latin for example, with two vertical strokes but rather with two horizontal ones:

The character for "ren" thus looks as follows:

Combining in this way the symbol for "human being" with the symbol for "two" shows quite unmistakably that true humanity can only be experienced in and through the relation to another human being. And it is this that is the essential thing for Confucius. "Humanity" is always a "co-humanity".[54] This means that, when seeing to the development of our own needs, wishes and goals, we must constantly bear in mind the development and the welfare of others. "Ren" comprises the obligation also to take on responsibility vis-à-vis other people:

Desiring to take his stand, one who is Good helps others to take their stand. Wanting to realize himself, he helps others to realize themselves.[55]

But what does this mean, concretely? What does it mean to "take one's stand" by "ren" and to help others to do so? Indeed, what precisely is "ren"? When a pupil posed this last question to him Confucius's answer was simply:

Care for others.[56]

"Ren", then, is in the first instance a feeling of love and concern or, in other words, the capacity for empathy and emotional participation in the lives and fates of other people. This first aspect of "ren" is something that we all have some experience of: for example through the empathetic and caring love of a mother for her child. But even powerful rulers, Confucius argues, must be able to "care for" their people in this way:

To guide a state of one thousand chariots [...] be frugal in your expenditures and cherish others.[57]

"Ren", however, also has a second aspect: a cognitive one. "True humanity" consists, for Confucius, not just in "love for one's neighbour" as a mere sense of empathy with this latter but, above and beyond this, in a conscious, rational decision to pursue the goal of bringing about the Good. It is possible for us to take a rational decision in favour of "ren" and to set about developing "ren" in the world in a precisely targeted way. "Humanity" in this sense is a maxim for our actions that we should strive to apply and bring to realization in all we do. When the pupil Zigong enquired of Confucius whether there was "one word that could serve as a guidance for one's whole life", Confucius replied:

Is it not "understanding"? Do not impose upon others what you yourself do not desire.[58]

Confucius poses here, for the first time, the demand that any action that can genuinely be called ethical and good must be generalisable, or "universalizable". That is to say, one's own actions can only be evaluated as "good" if one can also wish that everyone in the world should act according to the same maxim as oneself. Confucius, indeed, formulates this idea in the form of a negation, or in other words of a "not wanting to be treated wrongly"; but the core idea is the same:

Do not impose upon others what you yourself do not desire.[59]

Thirdly, "ren", in Confucius's writing, is a kind of court of decision, internal to each person, judging what is right and what is not. Every human being bears within him- or herself the possibility and the capacity to do what is right. In cases where "what is right" seems doubtful, what is needed to resolve the question is not just the "li", or the laws, the customs and the rites, nor just "xiao", or respect for the instructions imparted by parents and by state. What is needed is rather, above all, one's own inward self-examination:

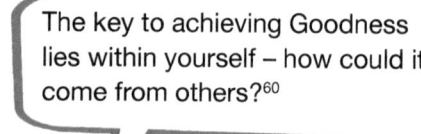

The key to achieving Goodness lies within yourself – how could it come from others?[60]

When he was asked by a pupil what "ren", or "true humanity" really meant, Confucius replied:

Restraining yourself and returning to the rites constitutes true humanity.[61]

The decisive thing here is that Confucius accords to every human being the capacity to "restrain themselves" and thereby to draw and develop out of themselves the virtue of "ren", or of true humane co-existence.

Confucius anticipates here very much of what the European philosopher Immanuel Kant was to formulate some 2300 years later in his "categorical imperative". Much as Kant was later to do, Confucius is saying that it depends on us ourselves alone whether or not we act in such a way that our action is so exemplary that it can become a basis for the action of every human being. The standard by which "right and wrong" are judged, or in other words the standard for "right action", is something that every human being carries within himself. Such a standard requires no help from outside authorities.

To sum up, then: "Ren", or "true humanity", has in Confucius's writing three different important meanings. Firstly, it consists in the feeling of empathy and love, i.e. the capacity to emotionally participate in the lives of others. Secondly, it consists in a conscious compliance with certain guidelines for action, or with the fundamental rule of reason whereby one should behave with regard to others in the same way as one would wish others to behave with regard to oneself.

Thirdly, "ren" is a kind of court of decision, internal to each person, which enables the distinguishing of good from bad action and thereby creates a duty to bring about the former rather than the latter:

To the gentleman duty is the guideline for his behaviour.[62]

This applies as much to the simple man of the people as it does to the ruler:

Desiring to take his stand, one who is good helps others to take their stand.[63]

Each individual should, if he is to be a "junzi" or true gentleman, think and act in an exemplary way, so that his behaviour can become a point of orientation for the behaviour of all others. For this reason, the means that such a man uses can never be in contradiction with the end: namely, true humanity:

Look at the means a man employs; observe the basis from which he acts.[64]

Confucius also rejects the death penalty, which at that time was still generally used, since it implicitly raises the possibility of killing to the status of a standard for action, something which contradicts the realization of "true humanity" as the highest of all principles. When a prince put the question to Confucius: "If I were to execute those who lacked the Way in order to advance those who possessed the Way, how would that be?"[65] Confucius drew his attention to the so-called Golden Rule and to his duty, as a prince, to himself behave in an exemplary manner:

Wieso müßt ihr töten, wenn ihr regiert? Ihr selbst müßt das Gute nur wirklich wollen, dann wird auch das Volk gut werden.[66]

He also reminds the prince of his duty to practice "ren" and to act exemplarily by always doing the right thing himself:

> To govern means to be correct. If you set an example by being correct yourself, who will dare to be incorrect?[67]

The ideal society, or the best of all possible governments, requires no death penalty, no corporal or capital punishment, nor even any prisons. Rather, such a society would rely wholly on "ren", on "true humanity":

> If you try to guide the common people with coercive regulations and keep them in line with punishments, the common people will become evasive and have no sense of shame.[68]

If, however, you guide them with virtue, and keep them in line by means of ritual, the people will have a sense of shame and will rectify themselves.[69]

"Ren', then, possesses a sort of "radiating" force. If it is practiced by the ruling government, and by the rulers themselves, in a decisive way, then it will have the almost magical effect of attracting others to practice it themselves:

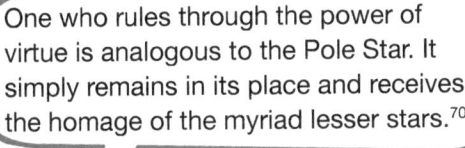

One who rules through the power of virtue is analogous to the Pole Star. It simply remains in its place and receives the homage of the myriad lesser stars.[70]

This very high valuation placed on "true humanity" as the highest standard and principle of action means, however, that "true humanity" also stands above the laws. If a law or a ritual clashes with the principle of "true humanity", it may be that one will have to refuse and resist this law or ritual. Confucius decidedly did not belong to the "Legalist" school of Chinese philosophers, who defined the strict observance of the law as the highest moral ideal. "Ren" stands above these. But what happens when rulers fail to rule according to the "Golden Rule" and the principle of "ren"? What is to be done when they follow rather immoral and selfish motives? Confucius's answer to these questions leaves no room for misunderstanding:

> No [...] good person would ever pursue life at the expense of goodness, and in fact some may be called upon to give up their lives in order to fulfil goodness.[71]

This means, in short, that it can sometimes be one's duty to resist when "ren" is infringed or disrespected. It follows that "li", or the rites and traditions of one's forefathers, and "xiao", or the piety which bids one obey one's parents, the government and the law, apply only so long as they prove to be compatible with "ren". When he was asked by his pupil Zi Lu how someone could become a "complete person" Confucius replied:

When seeing a chance for profit he thinks of what is right; when confronting danger he is ready to take his life into his own

hands; when enduring an extended period of hardship he does not forget what he had professed in more fortunate times – such a man might also be called a complete person.[72]

With this answer Confucius once again clearly enunciates the principle that we must be ready to take a stand in defence of our moral convictions. "Ren", in other words, ranks above "li" and "xiao". Where there is a conflict between one and the other, the individual must choose compliance with the principle of "true humanity" over allegiance to father, family or governmental authority. Because for the "true gentleman" a life spent striving constantly to realize "ren" is the very highest ideal. But Confucius would not be Confucius if he were not aware that this is a very, very high aim to set oneself and one which a human being can hardly hope to achieve even in a lifetime:

I have yet to meet a person who truly loved goodness or hated a lack of goodness.[73]

On another occasion he conceded that he was himself far from perfect:

How could I dare to lay claim to either sageliness or goodness. What can be said about me is no more than this: I work at it without growing tired and encourage others without becoming weary.[74]

But even if true and complete morality and humanity are difficult to achieve we must nonetheless try over and over to bring "ren" to realization. "Ren" is a lofty goal but is, in the end, not so far beyond our reach in our daily lives:

Is goodness really so far away? If I simply desire goodness, I will find that it is already here.[75]

Nevertheless, each individual must find his own way to goodness, be it as father of a family, farmer, teacher, craftsman, priest, official, musician or artist. And each of us is capable, Confucius is convinced, of fully realizing "ren", even if it is only for limited stretches of time, for example the length of a day:

Is there a person who can, for the space of a single day, simply devote his efforts to goodness (ren)?[76]

Confucius's central idea thus begins to take clearer shape. Each individual should strive, in his or her own way, strive to observe the "li", or the rules governing family and society, while also putting into practice the virtues of the "junzi" and thereby bringing "ren" to full realization. Confucius's great imperative runs: seek, in attempting to bring "ren" to realization, one's own "dao", or "right way", to doing so, that is, a way to live in harmony with one's fellow men and with oneself.

Find Your "Dao", Your "Right Way"! The Confucian Philosophy of Self-Cultivation

"Dao" is a complex and shifting concept, not only in Confucius's work but in the whole of Asian thought. Literally translated, "dao" means simply "way". But in its philosophical usage, both by Confucius and by the rival philosophical school the "Daoists", the term means "right way" or "proper way". In a metaphorical sense, then, it stands for "the right way to lead one's life":

Set your heart upon the Way, rely upon virtue (and) lean upon goodness [...].[77]

There is, indeed, a decisive difference between the way that the word "dao" is used in Confucius's writing and the way that it is used in the works of the so-called "Daoists", a mystical religious current of thought that enjoyed great popularity in Confucius's day. Following the ideas of Lao Zi, the legendary founder of their school, the Daoists saw in the "dao" a divinely established cosmic path which human beings were called upon to follow and by the following of which one could raise oneself to higher spiritual levels. If one succeeded, so these Daoists taught, in adapting oneself perfectly and completely to the natural rhythm of day and night, winter and summer, becoming and passing away, it is even possible to attain to a degree of physical and spiritual immortality. Confucius's notion of the "dao", however, is a precisely contrary one to this. For Confucius, it is not the divine cosmos that prescribes for Man the path to follow toward self-perfection. Rather, it is Man who, through his thoughts and deeds, perfects the cosmos:

Human beings can broaden the Way; it is not the Way that broadens human beings.[78]

Or, in an alternative translation:

Human beings can exalt the Way; it is not the Way that exalts human beings.[79]

For Confucius, that is to say, the "dao" does not have a divine but rather an ethical, practical dimension. One might indeed describe the entire philosophy of Confucius as "the search for the lost 'dao'". Confucius lived in an era of great political conflict and a general decline in public morality. China had fallen apart into a whole series of mutually hostile small states. Numerous influential noble families and clans had seized all power and determined arbitrarily what laws and rules were to apply on the particular bits of territory they had sway over. The common people felt deeply insecure and lived without placing any faith or trust in the state, with each man thinking only of his own interests and those of his immediate family. The goal pursued by Confucius was that of a return to a genuinely moral society, such as he

believed had existed under the legendary emperors
Yao, Shun and Yu:

Shun and Yu possessed the
entire world and yet had no
need to actively manage.[80]

It was clear to Confucius, however, that these exemplary rulers could never actually return in the flesh.
He was also fully aware that there were in his day,
and would always be, possessors of political power
who would have no inclination or desire to behave
morally. The ruler of the state of Qi at the time, for
example, ruled entirely without justice and directed
all his energies only to acquiring as many chariots as
possible, these latter being at the time the most important weapon of war:

Duke Jing of Qi had a thousand teams
of horses and yet on the day he died the
people could find no reason to praise him.[81]

So that the people would no longer have to rely merely on the good fortune of a benevolent ruler's hap-
pening to end up on the throne Confucius set about
looking for a timeless principle on which to base an
ethical order. He urged all citizens, and indeed all rulers, to behave with nobility in their daily lives and to
set about seeking, once again, for the "dao".

The "dao", then, for Confucius, means the right way
for the individual to live harmoniously with others
within society. It is the search for "ren", for "true humanity". But, being a search, it is not and cannot be
a pre-determined way but must rather be a principle for human action which we strive day by day to
bring to full realization. And it is only in the process
of bringing it to realization that we give to our exist-
ences a direction and a "way". All this, in fact, comes
to expression in the Chinese character for "dao". The
character does not, as one might expect, consist of
the image of a road or path but rather consists of two
signs.[82] These are the sign for "walking":

and, directly to the right of it, the sign for "head":

which gives, when put together:

This means that "the Way" really only becomes "the Way" when it is really travelled by the individual and, secondly, that "the true Way" arises only out of the interplay of head and foot, i.e. of acting and thinking. Acting and thinking, word and deed, belong together:

He first expresses his views and then acts in accordance with them.[83]

The two should always be in accord with one another. The "true Way", or the "dao", arises out of the inward and outward realization of the notion of "ren", or of "true humanity". Thus, whoever succeeds in attaining harmony with others shall have already set his foot on the path that leads in the right direction. It is necessary, indeed, in order to do this to have beforehand formed and cultivated one's character and one's comportment:

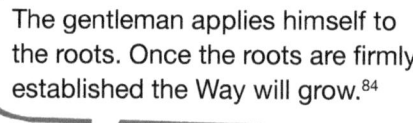

The gentleman applies himself to the roots. Once the roots are firmly established the Way will grow.[84]

For Confucius, then, the "dao", consisting as it does in the search for a harmonious society, is concerned at its core not with other-worldly but with worldly, political and ethical matters. But the school which took its name from this "dao", the so-called "Daoists", propounded a view which ran directly counter to this Confucian notion whereby a properly functioning social life formed a key building block for the "true Way". For the Daoists politics, state, state officials, rulers, cities, indeed civilization as a whole with all its rules, regulations and rituals was, in the last analysis, something contrary to Nature and did nothing but disturb the natural course of the cosmos.

Lao Zi one of the legendary founders of Daoism,[85] describes, in the famous work he is said to have authored, the Dao De Jing, the "dao" as "the principle that underlies the whole world", that is, as a kind of World-Reason or Law of the World. Generally in Nature, Lao Zi contended, everything spontaneously followed the "true Way". The only exception here was Man. In contrast to all the animals and plants Man had been thrown out of the natural course of things by his tendency to engage in cunning and greedy thought. Man wishes constantly to intervene, to change, to improve and to maximize his own advantage. But every such intervention, even if well-intentioned, tends to harm the natural course of the universe. Planning, calculating thought is thus, for the Daoists, the root of all evil, since it catapults Man out of Nature. Such things as technology, politics, morality and civilization take the place of the original oneness with Nature and alter and disturb the natural harmony.

Moreover, such human intervention was always unnecessary anyway, since, Lao Zi claims, the "dao" always orders and organizes itself. Every living being, plant or animal, has its own "dao", its own "right way", and wisdom consists simply in following it. There is even connected, in certain currents of Daoism, with this goal of living in Nature's rhythm, dissolving into Nature and even uniting with it a certain hope of eternal life. It is only logical, then, that the highest goal of the Daoists was "wu wei", meaning "non-doing". They lived, so far as possible, preferably very retiring lives, in monasteries, as hermits, or in small self-supporting communities. "Non-doing" meant, for them, an overcoming of one's own desire and will. Legend has it that Lao Zi once actually talked with Confucius and urged him to give up all his striving for just action, just government and just laws, since this striving, in the end, served only to disturb the way of Nature and the world. It is hard to imagine, however, Confucius ever losing his sense of an obligation to change the course of the world, since we are told that he said:

If the Way were realized in the world then I would not need to change anything.[86]

The contrast between Confucius and the Daoists can be clearly seen in the light of the following example: Once, when Confucius had to cross a river, he sent his pupil Zi Lu on ahead of him, who asked a local Daoist about the whereabouts of a ford where the river could be crossed. The Daoist replied that the famous and learned Confucius should really be familiar enough with the secrets of Nature to know where a river could best be crossed. After receiving this frustrating answer Zi Lu tried his luck with another local, also a Daoist. This latter, however, had no advice for him beyond that to withdraw, together with his master, from all commerce with the world and human beings. It is a better thing generally, this second Daoist urged, to trust to Nature and to have contact and conversation only with the birds and beasts of the forest. When Zi Lu reported this advice back to his master, Confucius's response was:

A person cannot flock together with the birds and the beasts. If I do not associate with the followers of men, then with whom would I associate?[87]

We can see here very clearly the contrast between the stance of Confucius and that of the Daoists. Confucius wishes to make the world a better place and is thereby obliged to have dealings with human beings. Becoming a hermit is not an option for him.

This contrast between Confucius and the Daoists is expressed in an even more poetic way in an old folk tale[88] which is still related in the Far East today. On another occasion when Confucius was travelling the country with his pupils he found his way blocked by a boy who had built a sand-castle in the middle of the road. On Confucius's asking, in astonishment, "will you not give way to us?" the boy replied: "wagons give way to cities, not cities to wagons".

When Confucius enquired as to his name and place of abode the boy said "I live without a name in the house of the wind", a reply generally understood to mean that the speaker was a Daoist who had made his home in Nature. Impressed by the boy's wit, Confucius invited him to come along with him, saying: "Let us put the world back in balance!" But to this the child gave, once again, a characteristically Daoist response: "What good would that do? If one bears away the mountains, where will the birds nest? If one fills up the seas, where will the fish live? The great world desires not to be put in balance." When Confucius proposed to the boy that he could, nonetheless, perhaps still have much to learn from him, an older and learned man, the boy questioned even whether this was the case. "Ask me something," replied Confucius. The boy asked him "How many stars shine in the sky?" Looking up and thinking for a while, Confucius said "Ask me rather about something closer to earth". The boy asked "How many hairs are there in your eyebrows?" At this Confucius gave up his attempts to make the boy his pupil, saying "Perhaps the younger generation does indeed surpass us". He bid his pupils to drive the wagon onward, taking care to go around the sand-castle in the middle of the road.

This story is another beautiful illustration of how,

whereas the Daoists found "the true Way" in the coming to be and passing away of Nature, this was an attitude that Confucius found it impossible to adopt. Confucius sought the "dao" not in spiritual harmony with the cosmos or in mystical union with the natural root of things but rather in a much more concrete, ethical harmony between human beings, that is, in the building up of a just society. Meditative contemplation of Nature, be it in monastery or idyllic landscape, was not enough for him. He wanted to set society in proper order:

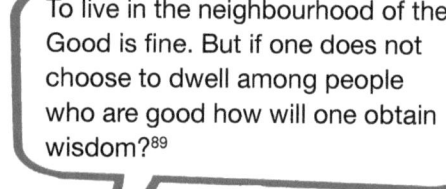
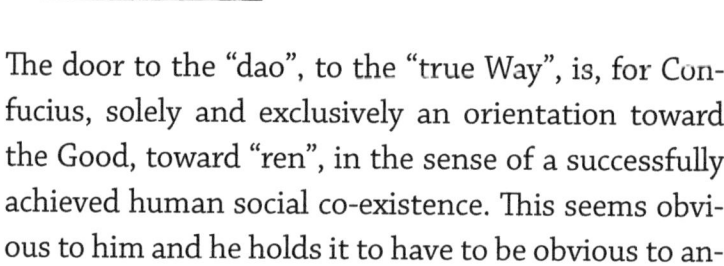

To live in the neighbourhood of the Good is fine. But if one does not choose to dwell among people who are good how will one obtain wisdom?[89]

The door to the "dao", to the "true Way", is, for Confucius, solely and exclusively an orientation toward the Good, toward "ren", in the sense of a successfully achieved human social co-existence. This seems obvious to him and he holds it to have to be obvious to anyone. The question torments him all the more, then:

> How is that no one follows (the right) Way?[90]

This problem of why human beings so seldom find the right Way was, in the end, the problem that occupied Confucius his whole life long. He never ceased to try to solve it but the idea of a meditative or ascetic withdrawal from the world was nothing he ever considered as a satisfactory solution. The enlightenment through meditative "all-in-oneness" recommended in Lao Zi's *Dao De Jing* was something that clearly did not suit Confucius's personality or constitution:

> I once engaged in thought for an entire day without eating and an entire night without sleeping but it did no good. It would have been better for me to have spent that time in learning (from others).[91]

It was only in conversation and in the living exchange of experiences with others, Confucius believed, that Man could find the "dao" or the "true Way".

Of What Use Is Confucius's Discovery for Us Today?

A Backward-Looking Teaching or a Timeless Truth? Confucius's Long Way

In the lands of the East thousands of generations have been deeply marked and formed by the basic demands made by Confucius on Man: self-improvement through education; harmony with family and state; and a society governed by morality, co-humanity and exemplary conduct. We also find in the daily life of many Asian societies the marks and traces of Confucius's conviction that, besides "li", or a nation's traditional rites and rituals, it is also and above all "ren", or actually lived-out and experienced "humanity", that holds society together. Still today millions of Chinese school pupils are taught to repeat the maxims of Confucius as part of their lessons, so as to thoroughly internalize their message. The history of Confucius's teachings in the Orient, however, is by no means as smooth a one as one might expect.

Confucius travelled with his pupils through the many small states which, in his age, filled the vast territory that is today the unified land of China and attempted to convince kings, princes and even entire populations of the truth of his teachings about the need to take a stand for true humanity. But only very few people really understood this doctrine, which was very much ahead of its time. Once, when Confucius's pupil Zi Lu, asked by a gatekeeper who he was, replied that he was a disciple of Confucius, the gatekeeper's response was: "Is that not the man who knows that his ideas can never be put into practice yet won't leave off teaching them anyway?"[92]

Confucius's ideas, and in particular the high moral demands that he made of rulers and his insistence that all people should be given access to education, made him a very suspicious character above all in the eyes of the kings and princes through whose lands he passed.

Some two hundred years after his death the rulers of the Qin dynasty even prohibited his doctrine entirely, as a sort of "heresy". As a deterrent to its propagation many Confucian scholars were executed. Some, it is said, were even buried alive.[93] In the year 213 BC the Qin emperor ordered the burning of all writings relating to him. Nevertheless, a few well-hidden copies survived the Qin persecution.

In the following, much more enduring dynasty, the Han (206 BC – 220 AD) Confucius's teachings rose again like a phoenix from the ashes. In the similarly long-lived Tang dynasty (618 AD – 907 AD) the *Lunyu* first became officially acknowledged as a "classic" and was thus incorporated into the material that had to be mastered by anyone taking the examination to qualify for high government service. From this point on Confucius was both a figure well-known to the common people and someone whose ideas constituted indispensable knowledge for the Chinese elites. That Confucian principle whereby one is not born a "junzi", or "gentleman" fit for high public office, but rather becomes one through education and character-formation, once perceived as "heretical", had become, a thousand years after Confucius's death, an element of official state doctrine:

To govern means to be correct.[94]

Precede the common people in accepting the burden of labour.[95]

In the year 687 AD it was finally ordained by the Emperor that temples to Confucius were to be erected in every city in China so that Confucius could be revered as "sheng ren", highest moral authority, indeed the sprit of morality itself, become man. The practice began of making sacrifices to Confucius's spirit of various types of food. Such practices continued right up until the end of the imperial system in China in 1911. Indeed, even in this period at the beginning of the 20th century when the last emperors of China were coming under increasing pressure to give way to democracy, they attempted to use Confucius to hold onto power. So as to distract and pacify the starving masses they solemnly declared Confucius to be not just a supremely moral man but an actual god. The people were given to understand that worshipping Confucius would bring them eternal life. The Chinese calendar was officially altered to make the year of Confucius's birth the year from which all dates were calculated. The temples and shrines to Confucius became places of veritable religious adoration and worship.

Confucius himself, of course, would have looked on all this with great displeasure because the truth he taught had very definitely been a truth "of this world". His teachings rest on argument, not on revelation. In his own lifetime he looked on himself neither as a god nor even as a saint or prophet. On the contrary, he said:

How could I dare lay claim to either sageliness or goodness?[96]

At bottom, both Confucius's person and his teachings were thoroughly rational and completely irreconcilable with every form of divine worship. Confucius, in other words, was a true agnostic. The Greek word *a-gnosis* means "not knowing" and Confucius, like the Agnostics of European antiquity, defends the view that all propositions that depend on the idea of the existence of God or gods must be classified as "not knowing", or as mere supposition. For Confucius, all that really matters is to do what is right in the "here below" of mortal daily life. This was the reason why he refused, his whole life long, to ever speak of God and preferred to speak only of "heaven" or "the heavens". When a pupil asked him directly how a person was to go about making contact with souls and spirits in heaven and how these souls and spirits could best be served his reply was

You are not yet able to serve people – how could you be able to serve ghosts and spirits?[97]

When the pupil insisted and began posing questions about existence after death, Confucius responded in a similar way:

You do not yet understand life – how could you possibly understand death?[98]

Confucius avoided, all his life, engaging in any speculation with his pupils about such things as "the world beyond". Thus, his pupil Zi Gong writes of him: "the Master's cultural brilliance is something one hears

about. But [...] one does not hear the Master ex-
pounding [...] on the ways of Heaven."[99] At another
point in the *Analects* we read: "The Master did not
discuss prodigies or [...] the supernatural".[100]

This brief period during which Confucius was wor-
shipped, much against the spirit of his own teaching,
as a literal god came to a sudden end when, in 1911,
the Chinese imperial system collapsed and, after
several revolts and revolutions, a republic was established in China. In this period, Confucius came to be
identified with the old feudal system and his ideas
rejected in their entirety for this reason. During the
so-called "May the Fourth movement" which began
in China immediately after World War One the slo-
gan was propagated "Smash the Confucius Store!"[101]
After a long period of civil and national wars the
Communist Party of China finally seized power in
the whole country. At the end of the 1950s its Party Chairman Mao Zedong urged a "Great Leap Forward" on his party comrades and on the nation as a
whole. China's teachers should thenceforth be Marx
and Lenin, no longer Confucius. Especially during
the even more radical period of the so-called Cultural
Revolution, which Mao launched a few years later in
the 1960s and 70s, Confucius came under attack as
a symbol of old and backward thinking. The young

Red Guards drawn from secondary and even primary schools took to singing mocking songs about Confucius, calling him a "rotten egg".[102] The temples to the great sage, which were now declared to be symbols of a rejected past, were scheduled for demolition. The order to tear them down, however, was followed in many regions only reluctantly and slowly and resistance to such measures reared its head even in the Communist Party itself. Mao Zedong, therefore, modified his orders to instructions that the temples, instead of being actively destroyed, should simply be left to crumble away naturally with time. This change of mind may have been symptomatic also of the rather ambivalent attitude Mao himself had toward Confucius.

At the age of 73 Chairman Mao drew worldwide attention to himself by swimming the Yangtze river at its broadest point, accompanied only by a few lifeguards. According to the press release Mao swam some 15 kilometres at a stretch, thereby proving that he was still filled with revolutionary energy. The poem that he wrote to commemorate this achievement cites, significantly, right in the middle of the text a line from Confucius's *Analects*:

Standing on the bank of a river, the Master said: "Look how it flows on like this, day and night!"[103]

Despite Mao's own continuing preoccupation with Confucius, however, Confucianism was forced, during these final years of Mao's leadership of China, to lead a sort of "shadow existence". Chinese intellectuals held Confucius responsible for the fact that China had, in recent centuries fallen far behind Western countries technically, culturally and economically. In neighbouring countries too, such as Vietnam and Korea, Confucian ideas were strongly criticized as being to blame for the persisting patriarchal backwardness in family structures and education, without a distinction really being made between the real historical Confucius and these ideas associated with his name.

This extremely negative evaluation changed when, in the two decades after Mao's death at the end of the 1970s, China began its rapid rise to the position of one of the world's leading economies and trading nations. We have recently seen the emergence, particularly from the side of Western sinologists and economists, of a thesis that is precisely the reverse of the old idea that Confucius's ideas were "holding China back". The consensus now is rather that the Confucian tradition of harmony and deep connection with family and state, profoundly anchored as it is in the Chinese people, has formed the real basis for the *tour de force* of rapid industrialization which has turned the Chinese economy, these last thirty or forty years, into one of the most dynamic in the world.

But in the end both these countervailing theories, one of which makes Confucius the backward-looking "brake" on economic development both in China and in the "Asian Tiger" economies, such as Taiwan, South Korea and Singapore, which had preceded it on this path, the other of which makes him the catalyst for just this rapid economic development, miss the essential point. In fact, Confucius's engagement for harmony in the sense of a truly and fully experienced co-humanity is neither an essentially backward-looking philosophy nor a guarantee for the creation of laborious, conforming, collectively thinking citizens. Confucius does indeed recommend that we seek harmonious equilibrium with others and that we always try to bear in mind the welfare of society as a whole. But he also demands of us that we fight with great determination for justice and true humanity when the principles of these latter are infringed. "Harmony", then, does not at all, for Confucius, mean the same thing as bowing unconditionally to the will of the collective; it also comprises contradicting and resisting this collective will:

No [...] good person would ever pursue life at the expense of goodness, and in fact some may be called upon to give up their lives in order to fulfil goodness.[104]

Despite all its emphasis on the notion of harmony, which does indeed still today play a great role in Asian thinking, the core of Confucius's philosophy was and is something quite different from what it is sometimes polemically described as: namely an "ethics of obedience", or even a "morality of slavery". On the contrary: what Confucius stands for is authenticity, truth and dialogue. Once, when one of his pupils asked him how a man might best "serve his lord", Confucius replied:

Do not deceive him.
Oppose him openly.[105]

Elsewhere in the *Analects* we find him saying:

In a state that is without the Way,
to be wealthy and honoured is
[...] a cause for shame.[106]

Confucius, then, was indeed "the thinker of harmony". But harmony as he conceived it essentially involved plain speaking and contradiction of one's fellow man, where necessary. Criticism, self-criticism and open dialogue and discourse are, for Confucius, vital elements in the bringing into being of "ren", or true humanity. In the last analysis, in other words, the doctrine defended by Confucius was a militant form of humanism that speaks to all ages and eras.

Perhaps this is why the doctrine has so magnificently stood the test of time. The house in the city of Qufu in which Confucius was born, and the temple dedicated to him that is attached to it, are today beloved tourist destinations attracting millions of visitors every year. The Master would surely be amused if he could see how, today, spoons, towels, postcards and powder-cases printed with his image are sold in enormous numbers. In 2004 the Chinese government decided to follow the example given by the German government with its "Goethe Institutes" or the Spanish government with its "Cervantes Institutes". It opened hundreds of educational institutions abroad with the declared aim of improving China's image as a nation with a great and important culture.

Whereas over the preceding twenty or thirty years it had primarily been as a suddenly hugely successful exporter of commercial products that China had attracted global attention, the plan was that the world should henceforth become acquainted with China's cultural achievements as well. And lo and behold, although it had originally been intended to name these worldwide Chinese cultural institutes after the great Communist leader Mao Zedong, it was in the end rather on Confucius that the choice fell. Today there are almost a thousand "Confucius Institutes" spread across all five continents.

The Miracle of the Axial Age: The Reordering of the World by Confucius, Buddha and Socrates

Confucius is one of the great thinkers of the so-called "Axial Age". This description "Axial Age" or, expressed more fully, "the empirically recognizable axis of world history"[107] is used by scholars, most famously perhaps by the German philosopher of history Karl Jaspers, to designate a certain epoch-making change or shift in which three world cultures, separately and independently, each took a great philosophical leap forward.

Thus, the period of Confucius's activity in China coincides almost exactly with that of the Buddha's activity in Northern India and Socrates's activity in Greece.[108] None of these three thinkers ever met any of the others, nor were they familiar with one another's teachings. But they were joined by an invisible band. Each of them was born into an era wracked by conflict and crisis and each completely altered the thinking of their milieu and age. It is in this period that human beings in different parts of the world come, almost simultaneously, to recognize for the first time that there are laws in Nature and that even human behaviour follows certain laws and that humanity needs to establish certain rules to guide and govern our co-existence. Jaspers speak of a first worldwide "Enlightenment" and of the birth, in this age, of what we today call "Reason". Knowledge now begins for the first time to play the foremost role in human life. It becomes clearly separated from non-knowledge. In a way reminiscent of Socrates's famous dictum "I know that I know nothing" we find Confucius saying

Do I possess wisdom? No, I do not [...] But I discuss problems from end to end until I get to the bottom of them.[109]

And, like Socrates, Confucius recommends:

This is wisdom: to recognize what you know as what you know and recognize what you do not know as what you do not know.[110]

In China as in Greece, then, the main concern suddenly became, in this period, that of distinguishing knowledge from superstition. This distinction lies at the origin of what, today, we call "science". If we accept the theory of the "Axial Age", then, the history of humanity falls clearly into two great epochs: the time before Confucius, Buddha and Socrates and the time after them. Prior to the intellectual revolution brought about by these three thinkers there had predominated, all over the world, "Nature"-religions, myths, shamanism and magic. Then come Confucius, the Buddha and Socrates, who dared to interpret and comprehend the world in terms that went beyond the archaic notions of gods of weather, harvest, war and fertility. They opened up to humanity an entirely new understanding of the world. Indeed, it was at this time that there arose those basic categories of thought which still characterize and form the very being of modern Man today.

Confucius, for example, might be said to anticipate, with his doctrine of harmony, humanity and the "Golden Rule", certain elements of Kant's "categorical imperative" and to sketch out, with his demand that we practice "ren" or "true humanity", an initial design for what later came to be called "humanism":

Do not impose upon others what you yourself do not desire.[111]

Socrates succeeded, with his so-called "maieutics", or "the technique of the midwife", in introducing into human practice a method of question and answer which did not presuppose any fixed result. And right up to the present day question and answer, argument and counter-argument, thesis and antithesis, trial and error, along with a logic which avoids self-contradiction form the basis of modern science.

Buddha, finally, introduces into human discourse, with his four truths and eightfold path to salvation, the idea that we need to rely neither on our material needs nor on a divine grace which will secure us a place in "the world beyond" but should rather seek our Way, our "dao", in the here and now, in the present world of our lives as we live them.

If we accept, then, the theory of the "Axial Age" we must recognize this age to have been the one in which humanity emerged from the twilight of Nature-worshipping religions into the light of that reason and self-knowledge which is still the ideal of modern Man.

The theory of the "Axial Age" remains indeed, like all such general theories of history, an object of some controversy. Cultural historians are by no means of one mind regarding either the dates of this "axial" period or the personalities involved.[112] It remains beyond doubt, however, that Confucius played a decisive role in this epoch-making reorientation of mankind and indeed continues to do so. With his teaching of harmony, co-humanity and the "Golden Rule" he provides mankind with an orienting principle that is valid for all ages.

Acquire Lightness with the Master: Self-Critique, Wit and Irony

Of what use is Confucius to us today? One aspect of Confucius's thought that tends to be neglected in the scholarly interpretations is the Master's characteristic lightness of spirit and wit:

In his leisure moments the Master was composed and yet fully at ease.[113]

But just this quality of being "at ease" was what made Confucius so human and is, perhaps, the quality most responsible for his ideas' having survived down the centuries and still being living ideas today. Even 2,500 years on we can still learn much from his light, easy attitude to life. Because despite the undeniable seriousness with which his appeal to be a "junzi", or a true noble "gentleman", is intended, Confucius was fully aware that most people – himself included – would never be able fully and constantly to meet the extremely high moral standards which he set:

Exerting myself to the utmost in performing funerary tasks, not allowing myself to be befuddled by wine – when have I ever fully succeeded in these things?[114]

The Master, his pupils testify, loved to smile and did so often. His philosophy, indeed, consists essentially in conversations with his pupils. It is true that there recurs again and again in these conversations Confucius's central idea: the search for harmony through the realization of "ren". But Confucius never developed any classically-constructed philosophical system comprising an ontology, an epistemology, a philosophy of history, an ethics etc. He was, in other words, not a "systematic philosopher". But this apparent failing is at the same time his strength and gives to his thinking something light, vibrant and unpredictable. Often, Confucius replies to the questions of his pupils with an ironic counter-question.

When, for example, a pupil told him of a man from Daxiang who had remarked to him that his master, Confucius, while possessing great knowledge, could not lay claim to having an outstanding talent for any particular art, Confucius smiled and said, with deep irony:

> What art, then, should I take up? Archery? Charioteering? I think I shall take up charioteering.[115]

An unexpected turn was also taken by a conversation with four pupils whom Confucius asked about their wishes for the future. The pupil Zilu gave a highly exemplary answer, saying that he would like best of all to be appointed minister in a state threatened by external enemies and disrupted from within by hunger and division. In just three years, he hoped, he would be able to solve all three problems. The second pupil too stated that he wished for some position in government in which he could apply all the knowledge he had acquired from Confucius. His desire, he said, was to give people courage through exemplary action and the passing of just laws. Then Confucius turned to Gong Xihua, the third pupil, asking:

What would you do?[116]

This latter replied, still very much in good Confucian style and spirit: "I am not saying that I would actually be able to do it but my wish, at least, would be to learn it. I would like to serve as a minor functionary, properly clad in cap and gown, in ceremonies at the ancestral temple, or at diplomatic gatherings."[117]

Finally, Confucius put the same question to the last of the four pupils, Zeng Xi. This last pupil was much more hesitant and reluctant to reply. He even excuses himself with the words: "I would choose to do something quite different from any of the other three."[118] Confucius, however, encourages him to speak, saying:

What harm is there in that? We are all just talking about our aspirations.[119]

Plucking up courage, then, the pupil says: "In the third month of spring, once the spring garments have been completed, I should like to assemble a company of five or six young men and six or seven boys to go bathe in the Yi river and enjoy the breeze upon the Rain Dance altar, and then return singing to the Master's house."[120] When Confucius heard this, he sighed and said:

I am with Zeng Xi.[121]

One needed, then, always to be prepared, with Confucius, for a completely unexpected answer. On one occasion his pupils were expecting to hear from the Master strong approval of Wen Zi, a high official from the state of Lu whom they imagined to be a perfect model because he was said to reflect three times before taking any action. Confucius's comment, however, was:

Twice would have been enough.[122]

Sometimes Confucius even recognized certain contradictions in his own teaching, although he was able also to explain and justify these. When, on one occasion, his pupil Zi Lu asked him whether he ought to apply within his own family those ethical principles that he had learned from the Master, Confucius replied that, given his youth, he ought to respect his parents and rather be reticent about making ethical proposals within the family. But when, a little later, the pupil Ran Qiu put to him the same question, Confucius was heard to say:

Upon learning of something that needs to be done, you should immediately take care of it.[123]

A third pupil, having heard, by chance, both these apparently mutually contradictory instructions, asked the Master whether he was not being inconsistent here. Confucius replied:

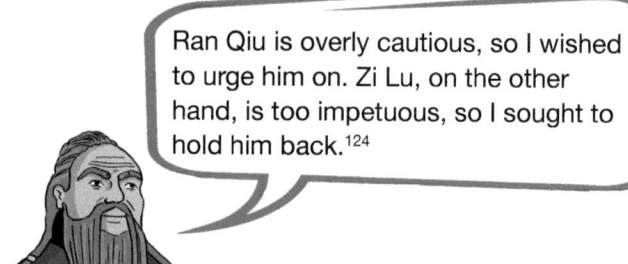

Ran Qiu is overly cautious, so I wished to urge him on. Zi Lu, on the other hand, is too impetuous, so I sought to hold him back.[124]

This answer shows that Confucius was not just a philosopher but also a very skilled psychologist. He always cherished the respective individualities of his pupils and took these individualities into account:

[Wisdom is] to know others.[125]

Very interesting in this connection is one episode in which Confucius himself came into conflict with the rites and rituals. He had been invited by a very unpleasant and corrupt government official to a personal interview in the ruler's palace. The official in question clearly wanted to use the distinction of a visit from Confucius to his advantage. Confucius, however, felt no inclination to make this visit to the palace, since he despised the official concerned. In terms of "li", however, or proper rites and traditions, he was under an ethical obligation to accept this invitation. Confucius, then, initially adopted a very diplomatic way of refusing it. He pointed out that the tradition was that the person who wished to meet with another person should be the one to make the journey to the desired meeting, so that it was not right that he, Confucius, should come to the palace. And when the insistent official did actually make the journey to see Confucius, the Master had him informed by a servant, when he was already making his way up the stairs of the house, that he was ill and could receive no one. Confucius, however, "then picked up his zither and sang, making sure that he could be heard".[126] In this way, Confucius at the same time respected the rituals and traditions while proclaiming, through his joyful song, the real truth.

Confucius was a fascinating personality. And perhaps we should learn to adopt something of his lightness and rhetorical agility. Often, the most sensible thing to do does indeed appear to be: to respond to a question with a good counter-question, so as to open up space for discussion. Above all, it is certainly the case that, especially in moral questions, a certain modesty and ability to ironize about ourselves such as were practiced by Confucius can protect us from the danger of over-estimating our own capacities. Precisely when we are making moral demands of others it can certainly do no harm to ask, with Confucius, the question:

When have I ever fully succeeded in these things?[127]

Opposing is a Form of Esteeming

Another part of the legacy of Confucius which can be very useful in practical life is his encouragement to adopt a stance of opposition and contradiction. What Confucius is concerned with here is not just our correcting, where necessary, certain untruths that may be advanced by others but, above all, our learning to appreciate corrections and contradictions that our conversation partners may feel moved to make to whatever it is we ourselves are saying. Nowadays, someone's correcting, contradicting or criticizing us is often all too readily construed as something negative, degrading or lacking in due respect. When such things occur we have a tendency to become defensive and to stick all the more stubbornly to the opinion our conversation-partner wishes to contradict or critique. We want to be "right at all costs" and to defend our status as "someone who knows". But this attitude is entirely the wrong one to take. Confucius teaches us to take an entirely different approach to opposition and contradiction. When a friend, for example, does not hesitate to speak plainly with us and to tell us some "hard home truths" about how we might do things better or differently, truths which we are unable maybe to fully perceive from our own perspective, this is not an attack on us but an expression of esteem:

If you are really dutiful toward someone, can you then fail to instruct him?[128]

Good friends prove that they are good friends precisely by being able to say anything at all to one another. This includes expressing contrary views and truths uncomfortable for the other party, since each true friend knows that the other is respectful, at bottom, of their personality and that any criticism that is made is made on just this foundation. The criticism does not endanger this foundation but, on the contrary, strengthens and deepens it. Someone who never says anything that might offend us and agrees with everything we say may be someone who causes no problems in our life; but neither does such a person help us to learn or improve ourselves in any way. A harmony between friend and friend, or between teacher and pupil, or between partners in a relationship, that is borne by a permanent harmony can even be a dangerous thing. Thus, Confucius says of his most gifted pupil Yan Hui, who was some thirty years his junior, that he had the most rapid comprehension of all and most resembled the Master in his thinking but that precisely this was regrettable in him:

Yan Hui is of no help to me. He is pleased with everything I say.[129]

It is important that one be contradicted, if one is to further develop one's thoughts and sharpen them.

Confucius even recommended that "yea-sayers" be avoided:

Befriending clever flatterers, skilful dissemblers, or the smoothly glib – these are the harmful types of friendship.[130]

Although Confucius accorded great importance to children honouring and respecting their parents, he even conceded that opposition and contradiction were permissible here:

In serving your parents you may gently remonstrate with them.[131]

Also, and indeed above all, in politics contradiction and opposition are important, in cases where rulers make wrong or unjust decisions:

If what the ruler says is good and no one opposes him, is this not good? On the other hand, if what he says is not good and no one opposes him, does this not come close to being a single saying that can cause a state to perish?[132]

In the end, what Confucius teaches us is something very simple: that we should control our vanity and not consider every contrary opinion as a personal insult. Frank and honest opposition is not a degradation of one's conversation partner but rather, on the contrary, a way of esteeming him or her.

Confucius's Legacy – the Lifelong Search for the Dao

Of what use is Confucius for us today? Especially irresistibly fascinating for our contemporary world is Confucius's recommendation, made some 2,500 years ago, that one should seek, every day anew, for the "dao" or the "true Way":

The gentleman devotes his thoughts to attaining the Way, not to obtaining food.[133]

Be sincerely trustworthy and love learning, and hold fast to the good Way until death.[134]

In the West, it has only been since the emergence first of the Enlightenment and then of Marxism, psychoanalysis and Existentialism that the question of the "dao", the right way to live one's life, has really come to the fore. Because it is really such thinkers as Hobbes, Rousseau, Marx, Freud, Sartre and Heidegger who pose, in the Western world, for the first time the question of the right path leading to the "self-realization of the individual in the community", of "the development of the individual as species-being", or of the possibility of an "authentic existence". In the Middle Ages these questions remained unposed in Europe, since the answers had already been given by church and religion. Man, people were told, had to fear God, follow the Ten Commandments, and resist all temptations, so as to enjoy eternal life after death. Confucius could not agree with this notion of the "true Way"'s having been instituted as a kind of test for admission into Paradise. For Confucius, this "Way" is not pre-established by some metaphysical or divine principle but must rather be created by us ourselves, through our words and deeds:

Human beings can broaden the Way; it is not the Way that broadens human beings.[135]

Put simply: Man can "broaden", that is, give specific moral form to his Way through good actions but there is no divinely pre-established Way that can give moral form to Man. For Confucius, we need rather to actively concern ourselves, every day anew, about our "dao", our self-cultivation, and our further self-development. We do indeed make mistakes here. Sometimes we tell a lie, big or small, to get ahead;

other times we develop in the wrong direction; or we betray ourselves or offend others. But this is all part of life. No one, says Confucius, is born a saint and no one succeeds in always doing the right thing. The important thing is just to learn something that will help with the next steps on the road:

To make a mistake and yet to not change your ways – this is what is called truly making a mistake.[136]

"The goal is the Way": this saying is often ascribed, on the Internet and in various books and magazines, to Confucius. He never formulated it in this way. But the thought doubtless does indeed correspond to one of his key ideas. Confucius was a pragmatic spirit and knew that human beings needed to concern themselves, day by day, with their "dao":

The key to achieving goodness lies within yourself – how could it come from others?[137]

When, after more than a thousand years of unbroken Confucian tradition, the Confucians first encountered Christian missionaries in the 17th century each were astonished at the beliefs of the other. It was, so to speak, a "clash of civilizations". This "clash" is very graphically expressed in some letters supposedly written back to the Chinese Emperor by his ambassador in Europe. They describe this ambassador taking part in a Roman Catholic mass and noting how, at the height of the ceremony, the priest raised the bread and wine, blessed them, and intoned: "this is my body and my blood, which was shed for all your sins". He then observed how the priest drank a sip of the wine and ate of the bread before offering both to the congregation so that they too might partake of God's power and spirit.

The ambassador then wrote to the Emperor in the following terms: "When they have made a god, they eat him up. The great Confucius would have found such a mode of divine worship repulsive and ridiculous."[138] This description of the clash between Catholic liturgy and Confucianism was, however, consciously composed as a way of critiquing the former. It, and the letters it is drawn from, were not really written by a Chinese ambassador but by Frederick the Great, the King of Prussia. Frederick was, in fact, a great admirer of Confucius and hoped, by making use of the Chinese philosopher's eminently rational persona, to expose Catholicism as a superstition.

But even if what is described in the letter is not real, it has a core of truth. Confucius would indeed have observed the mass with incomprehension, puzzlement, or at the least a smile of amusement. He esteemed, indeed, rituals performed to honour ancestors but the ritual consumption of a god would certainly have been, in his eyes, going too far. Despite his great appreciation of the "li", or the rites and customs, Confucius was always, at bottom, concerned to establish the use and purpose of these rites and customs in achieving harmony in society. His teachings were focussed firmly on the co-existence of human beings in the world "here below". The problems, he argued, were to be solved here in this world without trying to bring any "higher power" into play.

This attitude has left a lasting mark on the Far East. Even today the Chinese, for example, celebrate their most important festival, the New Year festival, with a ritual commemoration of the ancestors such as was already practiced at the time of Confucius. It is not a matter here of divine worship or of the hope of eternal life but rather simply of reverence for their forefathers and the appreciation of what earlier generations have done for present-day mankind. The Far East, in other words, remains Confucian and "this-worldly". Not surprisingly, then, all the attempts made by Jesuits in the 17th century to "convert" the Chinese failed. Unlike in Africa and the Americas, Christianity failed to take root in China. The wisdom best accepted there remained the Confucian one of:

Respecting the ghosts and spirits while keeping them at a distance.[139]

Confucius's central idea of harmony and the realization of a peaceful society of "true gentlemen" based on "this-worldly" values was criticized, right up to the 19th century, by Christians as a vision lacking in faith and true religious feeling. European philosophers such as Hegel and Kant also complained that Confucianism lacked metaphysical depth. And it is certainly true that, right from the start, Confucianism has something pragmatic and restrained about it. That development of his philosophy which was given to it by later philosophers after Confucius is still today known by the name of "Ru Jia", meaning both "the school of the learned" and "the school of the gentle".[140] It is certainly accurate to describe Confucius and the tradition of thought derived from his teachings as "gentle", inasmuch as the absence of religious pathos also means an absence of eschatological drama.

It was, for example, perhaps for just this reason that Confucius's ideas could never be used to justify war. His teachings could never be instrumentalized in the way that Western religions were being instrumentalized, on the other side of the world, to justify bloody wars. The Christian Crusaders rode into battle crying "Deus lo vult!" ("God wishes it!")[141] just as Muslim warriors cried, often in battle against these very Christians, on their side "Allahu Akbar!" ("God is the Greatest!"). But it has never happened, and is simply impossible to imagine, that an army should march into battle chanting "Confucius says..."

But even Confucius, of course, has now and then, in the course of the centuries, been misused by the powerful for their own ends. And, just like the doctrines of Jesus, Buddha or Mohammed, Confucius's doctrine remains a timeless ideal which has never been fully and perfectly realized. Unlike these doctrines, however, what Confucius teaches us about how to live our lives has a pragmatic core and remains firmly focussed on the world "here below". Perhaps it is precisely this modest, humanity-focussed attitude that is the most important part of his legacy to us today. What Confucius urges on us is, in the end, a pragmatic humanism. He promises no salvation; but neither does he condemn us to Hell for our human failings. It is enough, from his viewpoint, that we work to correct these failings:

If you have committed a transgression, do not be afraid to change your ways.[142]

The Way itself is the goal. And the Way sometimes demands that we correct ourselves. A stubborn "standing on principle" is never appropriate:

The gentleman is true, but not rigidly trustworthy.[143]

Change is important. But we should begin with ourselves:

Only the [...] very stupid do not change.[144]

As a wandering scholar with his characteristic beard and moustache it is easy to associate Confucius with the feudalistic age of autocratic rulers, loyal subjects and superstition in which he lived. But the message conveyed by the thoughts he developed is a timeless one. Reformulated in modern terms, this message consists in the five following points:

Demand much of yourself but ask little of others.[145]

Firstly: Nobody is perfect – there will always be human failings and there will always be crises. The important thing is to learn from them!

Secondly: If something does not seem right to you, you must take steps to change it. Begin with yourself and strive to be an example to others.

Thirdly: Be concerned with your own education and self-development but see to it that others also have the opportunity to develop.

Fourthly: Respect the existing laws and customs but speak out against them in every case where they are injurious or lack true humanity. Take a stand in defence of your convictions, if necessary at the risk of your life.

Fifthly: Search, every day anew, for your "dao"; live out your own humanity and never deviate from it!

It is, of course, an extremely difficult thing to do completely adequate justice to all five of these exhortations, particularly those involving the realization of true humanity and the ensuring that others too have their chance for self-development. Confucius himself recognized this, saying:

And he continues, regretfully:

Indeed, he conceded that even he himself had never succeeded in setting aside his own ego to a degree sufficient to live constantly in harmony with the world and his fellow men and to behave exemplarily after the manner of a "junzi" or "true gentleman":

> There is no one who is my equal when it comes to cultural refinement; but as for actually becoming a gentleman in practice, this is something that I have not yet been able to achieve.[148]

But it is precisely this, his modest and sceptical assessment of the moral capacities of Man, that makes Confucius so appealing. Even his scepticism, however, did not prevent him from developing his own great moral vision. Despite all the selfishness and confessed personal weaknesses that characterize Man, Confucius nonetheless insists that the possibility and opportunity exist for us to persistently bear in mind the welfare of other individuals and the good of society as a whole. Humanity can, and should, be actual lived humanity. This is the core of Confucius's message – a message which is valid for all times and places: nobody is perfect; no one is a saint. We are, indeed, not morally bound to be saints; but this does not mean that we should not persist, our whole lives long, in searching for the "dao", the "True Way". Once, when a pupil asked him whether he could sum up in a single sentence just what the "dao" was, Confucius replied:

"Is that all?" asked the pupil.

Bibliographical References

1   Confucius, Analects (With Selections from Traditional Commentaries), translated by Edward Slingerland, Hackett Publishing Company, Indianapolis/Cambridge, 2003, Chapter IV, 1, p. 29.
2   Confucius's actual birth-name was Kong Qiu, that is to say, "Qiu from the family Kong". He himself sometimes refers to himself, in the Analects, as "Qiu". In the Chinese literature, however, the polite form of address "Kong Fuzi", meaning "Master Kong" or "Teacher Kong", is mostly used. The name he is known by in the West, Confucius, is an attempt by this first (Jesuit Christian) translators to reproduce this Chinese name in the Latin form which they were accustomed to using in their writing.
3   The Analects originate in the various notes and transcriptions made by pupils of Confucius during the several decades of his teaching activity. Several different transcribers and several different periods have been distinguished within the text. The edition most relied on by scholars today is based on a synthesis of the various source texts put together by Confucian scholars between the 3rd and the 1st century BC. One important source here was a 21-chapter compendium, written in old-style characters, discovered within the walls of the ancestral home of the Kong family at one time inhabited by Confucius himself. It was discovered during the reign of the Emperor Jing (157-141 BC), i.e. three hundred years after the death of Confucius, having survived unscathed the great persecution of Confucians, involving a great book-burning, during the Qin dynasty (221-206 BC).
4   Confucius, Analects (With Selections from Traditional Commentaries), translated by Edward Slingerland, Hackett Publishing Company, Indianapolis/Cambridge, 2003, Chapter IV, 15, p. 34.
5   Ibid. Chapter XV, 12, p. 179.
6   Ibid. Chapter XIII, 23, p. 149.
7   Ibid. Chapter XV, 24, p. 183.

8   For a long time, before the ideas of Confucius were introduced into the West, it was generally believed in Europe that it was the Bible – specifically, Luke 6.31, which contains the famous line "do unto others as you would have them do unto you" – that had been the sole source and origin of the "golden rule". It came as a great surprise that Confucius had formulated the same idea five hundred years before the early Christians. The actual term "golden rule", indeed, is not biblical but was introduced by Anglican Christians at the beginning of the 16th century.

9   Ibid.

10   Ibid. Chapter XIV, 28, p. 165.

11   Ibid. Chapter XV, 36, p. 188. The English text has been revised here. It runs, in fact, "When it comes to being good..." But the term used in the Chinese original is "ren", "humanity".

12   Ibid. Chapter IX, 6, p. 88.

13   Whether, and if so for how long, Confucius really did work as minister for the ruler of the small Chinese state of Lu remains a question disputed by scholars. Some researchers have suspected that Confucians of later times may have invented and interpolated this episode in his biography so as to reinforce the idea that he had been an important political figure experienced in the practical handling of such questions. What remains indisputable is that certain of his pupils did indeed hold such high offices and that he himself would at least have been ready and willing to take such an office on. We find him saying in the Analects "If someone would simply employ me, within a single year I could put things into some kind of order, and within three years the transformation would be complete" (XIII, 10, p. 144). Much suggests, however, that Confucius never held any such office at all. For example, we also read in the Analects: "Do not be concerned that you lack an official position [...] Do not be concerned that no one has heard of you but rather strive to become a person worthy of being known" (IV, 14, p. 34). The most reliable source for the reconstruction of Confucius's biography remains the substantial chapter on him in the historical annals of the great historian Si Maqian who, admittedly, lived centuries after the philosopher in the Han dynasty.

14   Confucius, Analects (With Selections from Traditional Commentaries), translated by Edward Slingerland, Hackett Publishing Company, Indianapolis/Cambridge, 2003, Chapter II, 7, p. 10.

15   Ibid. Chapter XII, 11, p. 130.
16   Ibid. Chapter VI, 29, p. 63. What is meant here is that a ruler should behave as is appropriate for a ruler, a subject as is appropriate for a subject etc. It does not imply that any individual is permanently trapped in his assigned position, since a "son", for example, can later become a "ruler" etc.
17   Ibid. Chapter II, 21, p. 15.
18   Ibid. Chapter II, 23, p. 15.
19   Ibid. Chapter III, 7, p. 20.
20   Ibid. Chapter VIII, 8, p. 80.
21   Ibid. Chapter III, 4, p. 18.
22   Ibid. Chapter XI, 16, p. 117.
23   Confucius, Analects, in Chinese Classics, Volume One, translated by James Legge, Hong Kong, London, 1861, p. 86. The Classical Chinese of the Analects is an extremely compressed language and therefore open to a very wide range of alternative interpretations and translations. The modern translation by Slingerland, for example - which has been the translation principally used in the present book - interprets this passage as having a sense which is the very opposite to the sense conveyed by the lines quoted here, which have been taken from Legge's older translation. (Slingerland has Confucius claiming rather that "these sorts of things present me with no trouble", thus presenting himself as indeed a moral model for others). It seems to the present author that Legges's interpretation is the more plausible, so it is the Legge reading that is cited here.
24   Confucius, Analects (With Selections from Traditional Commentaries), translated by Edward Slingerland, Hackett Publishing Company, Indianapolis/Cambridge, 2003, Chapter V, 27, p. 51.
25   Ibid. Chapter XVII, 2, p. 200.
26   Ibid. Chapter IV, 5, p. 31.
27   Ibid. Chapter I, 8, p. 3.
28   Ibid. Chapter I, 14, p. 6.
29   Ibid. Chapter XVII, 6, p. 202.
30   Ibid. Chapter I, 1, p. 1.
31   Ibid. Chapter I, 8, p. 3.
32   Ibid. Chapter IX, 24, p. 94.
33   Ibid. Chapter XIV, 27, p. 165.
34   Ibid. Chapter VI, I, p. 58.

35   Ibid. Chapter XIII, 3, p. 139.
36   Ibid.
37   Ibid. Chapter VII, 8, p. 66.
38   Ibid. Chapter XIII, 28, p. 149.
39   Ibid. Chapter XIII, 13, p. 144.
40   Ibid. Chapter XV, 21, p. 182.
41   Ibid. Chapter XV, 2, p. 174.
42   Ibid. Chapter I, 1, p. 1.
43   Ibid. Chapter 15, 39, p. 189.
44   Ibid. Chapter VII, 7, p. 67.
45   Ibid. Chapter XI, 1, p. 111.
46   Ibid. Chapter 16, 9, p. 196.
47   Ibid. Chapter 7, 20, p. 71.
48   Ibid. Chapter 7, 22, p. 71.
49   Ibid. Chapter 2, 11, p. 11.
50   Ibid. Chapter 2, 15, p. 13.
51   Ibid. Chapter 17, 8, p. 203.
52   Ibid. Chapter 13, 5, p. 141.
53   Ibid. Chapter 13, 28, p. 149.
54   The Confucius expert Xuewu Gu even recommends that the word "ren"
     be translated directly as "co-humanity", since this would come closer
     to Confucius's intentions than the usual translations as "humanity",
     "moral behaviour", "love of one's neighbour", "benevolence", "good-
     ness" etc. The character "ren" is very old and was used, for centuries,
     to mean every kind of goodness. But it was Confucius who first gave
     to it the specific philosophical significance of "a form of behaviour
     aimed at successful co-existence with others".
55   Confucius, Analects (With Selections from Traditional Commentaries),
     translated by Edward Slingerland, Hackett Publishing Company, Indi-
     anapolis/Cambridge, 2003, Chapter VI, 30, p. 63.
56   Ibid. Chapter 12, 22, p. 136.
57   Ibid. Chapter 1, 5, p. 2.
58   Ibid. Chapter 15, 24, p. 183.
59   Ibid. Chapter 12, 2, p. 126.
60   Ibid. Chapter 12, 1, p. 125.
61   Ibid. (translation slightly altered).
62   Ibid. Chapter 16, 13, p. 199.
63   Ibid. Chapter 6, 30, p. 63.

64 Ibid. Chapter 2, 10, p. 11.
65 Ibid. Chapter 12, 19, p. 134.
66 Ibid.
67 Ibid. Chapter 12, 17, p. 133.
68 Ibid. Chapter 2, 3, p. 8.
69 Ibid.
70 Ibid. Chapter 2, 1, p. 8.
71 Ibid. Chapter 15, 9, p. 177.
72 Ibid. Chapter 14, 12, p. 158.
73 Ibid. Chapter 4, 6, p. 31.
74 Ibid. Chapter 7, 34, p. 76.
75 Ibid. Chapter 7, 30, p. 74.
76 Ibid. Chapter 4, 6, p. 31.
77 Ibid. Chapter 7, 6, p. 65.
78 Ibid. Chapter 15, 29, p. 185.
79 Ibid.
80 Ibid. Chapter 8, 18, p. 84.Yao, Shun and Yu were three emperors to whom there were attached many myths and legends, supposed to have reigned peacefully and justly over China in the third millennium before Christ.
81 Ibid. Chapter 16, 12, p. 196.
82 The Chinese character for "dao" consists of the radical "shou", which is used for "head", and the radical "chou", which is used to mean "walk" or "stamp with the foot". The "right way", then, emerges symbolically out of the interplay of head and foot, thinking and acting. "Radicals" in this sense are extremely ancient "root signs" which are put together in various combinations so as to form the basis of more complex signs. The "radicals" in Chinese traditionally number 214 but the total number of Chinese characters amounts to somewhere around 100,000.
83 Confucius, Analects (With Selections from Traditional Commentaries), translated by Edward Slingerland, Hackett Publishing Company, Indianapolis/Cambridge, 2003, Chapter 2, 13, p. 12.
84 Ibid. Chapter 1, 2, p. 1.
85 Lao Zi is said to have lived in the same era as Confucius, i.e. the fifth or sixth century BC. He was the legendary philosopher and author of the Dao De Jing, an 82-chapter collection of mystical texts and aphorisms which became one of the most important foundations of

Daoism. It has, however, never proven possible to definitively prove his authorship of this text or even that he really lived. His name is variously written Lao Zi, Lao Tse or Lao Tzu.

86 Confucius, Analects (With Selections from Traditional Commentaries), translated by Edward Slingerland, Hackett Publishing Company, Indianapolis/Cambridge, 2003, Chapter 18, 6, p. 217.
87 Ibid.
88 Cited in the German translation of the Analects by Volker Zotz.
89 Confucius, Analects (With Selections from Traditional Commentaries), translated by Edward Slingerland, Hackett Publishing Company, Indianapolis/Cambridge, 2003, Chapter 4, 1, p. 29.
90 Ibid. Chapter 6, 17, p. 58.
91 Ibid. Chapter 15, 31, p. 186 (translation slightly altered).
92 Ibid. Chapter 14, 38, p. 169.
93 See Ursula Grafe's postface to Die Weisheit des Konfuzius, Insel, Frankfurt am Main, 1964.
94 Confucius, Analects (With Selections from Traditional Commentaries), translated by Edward Slingerland, Hackett Publishing Company, Indianapolis/Cambridge, 2003, Chapter 12, 17, p. 133.
95 Ibid. Chapter 13, 1, p. 138.
96 Ibid. Chapter 7, 34, p. 75.
97 Ibid. Chapter 11, 12, p. 115.
98 Ibid.
99 Ibid. Chapter 5, 13, p. 44 (translation slightly altered).
100 Ibid. Chapter 7, 21, p. 71. Confucius uses the word "heavens" in several different senses in his reported lessons. Sometimes it refers to Nature, sometimes to society as a whole, to the universe or to Fate. But nowhere is it used by Confucius in the sense that it bears in, say, Christianity or Islam: a "paradise" to which we go after death if we have lived a good life.
101 The May the Fourth movement began with protests by students and other intellectuals against the Versailles Treaty which, although China had fought on the side of the Allies in the just-ended war, handed the territory around Shandong previously controlled by the defeated Germans not back to China but to the Japanese. For these modernizing young Chinese nationalists, Confucius was perceived as symbolizing the old feudal system which had led to such national

humiliation. See, for example, Gregor Paul, Konfuzius und der Konfuzianismus, Darmstadt, 2010.

102 Ibid.

103 Confucius, Analects (With Selections from Traditional Commentaries), translated by Edward Slingerland, Hackett Publishing Company, Indianapolis/Cambridge, 2003, Chapter 9, 17, p. 92.

104 Ibid. Chapter 15, 9, p. 177.

105 Ibid. Chapter 14, 22, p. 163.

106 Ibid. Chapter 8, 13, p. 82.

107 See Karl Jaspers "On the Origin and Goal of History", Yale University Press, 1953. Jaspers saw as such an "axis point in human history" the period from around 800 BC to around 200 BC. This by reason of the fact that, during these few centuries, three mutually independent human cultures miraculously make enormous progress in a short time and thereby provide the intellectual foundation on which even contemporary humanity still draws. Jaspers writes: "The fact of the threefold manifestation of the Axial Period is in the nature of a miracle, insofar as no really adequate explanation is possible within the limits of our present knowledge. [...] Really to visualize the facts of the Axial Period [...] is to gain possession of something common to all mankind, beyond all differences of creed." Ibid. pp. 18-19.

108 Although the Buddha's birth cannot be precisely dated we may assume that he lived around 500 BC, i.e. more or less contemporaneously with Confucius (551-479 BC) and Socrates (469-399 BC). Socrates, in other words, was born around ten years after Confucius's death.

109 Confucius, Analects (With Selections from Traditional Commentaries), translated by Edward Slingerland, Hackett Publishing Company, Indianapolis/Cambridge, 2003, Chapter 9, 8, p. 89 (translation slightly altered).

110 Ibid. Chapter 2, 17, p. 13.

111 Ibid. Chapter 15, 24, p. 183.

112 Already long before Jaspers the 18th-century French author Anquetil-Duperron had observed that Zarathustra, Confucius and Pherecydes had been contemporaries and had brought about "a kind of revolution" simultaneously in three separate parts of the world. Besides Confucius, Buddha and Socrates, Zarathustra, Lao Zi, Plato and Aristotle are often also mentioned in theories of an "axial age".

The scholar of antiquity Jan Assmann has carried out a general study of all the various theories of an "Axial Age" and come to the conclusion that, although the contention that such an age existed is not fully supported by unitary scientific findings, the theory nonetheless represents "a plea in favour of cosmopolitan humanism which rests on an certain realities "indeed common to all cultures". See Jan Assmann, Achsenzeit: Eine Archaeologie der Moderne, Munich 2018.

113 Confucius, Analects (With Selections from Traditional Commentaries), translated by Edward Slingerland, Hackett Publishing Company, Indianapolis/Cambridge, 2003, Chapter 7, 4, p. 65.
114 Ibid. Chapter 9, 16, p. 92 (translation altered).
115 Ibid. Chapter 9, 2, p. 86.
116 Ibid. Chapter 11, 26, p. 123.
117 Ibid.
118 Ibid.
119 Ibid.
120 Ibid.
121 Ibid.
122 Ibid. Chapter 5, 20, p. 48.
123 Ibid. Chapter 11, 22, p. 119.
124 Ibid.
125 Ibid. Chapter 12, 22, p. 136.
126 Ibid. Chapter 17, 20, p. 208 (translation altered).
127 Ibid. Chapter 9, 16, p. 92 (translation altered).
128 Ibid. Chapter 14, 7, p. 156.
129 Ibid. Chapter 11, 4, p. 112.
130 Ibid. Chapter 16, 4, p. 194.
131 Ibid. Chapter 16, 4, p. 194.
132 Ibid. Chapter 13, 15, p. 145.
133 Ibid. Chapter 15, 32, p. 187.
134 Ibid. Chapter 8, 13, p. 82.
135 Ibid. Chapter 15, 28, p. 187.
136 Ibid. Chapter 15, 30, p. 186.
137 Ibid. Chapter 12, 1, p. 125.
138 These fictional letters were actually composed by the Prussian king, Frederick the Great, under the title "Reports of Phihihu, Ambassador of the Chinese Emperor to Europe". Frederick in fact admired Confucianism as an exemplary rationalism, as did his "court philosopher"

Voltaire. After having read Confucius, he composed the letters as a way of criticizing the Catholic Church.

139 Confucius, Analects (With Selections from Traditional Commentaries), translated by Edward Slingerland, Hackett Publishing Company, Indianapolis/Cambridge, 2003, Chapter 6, 22, p. 60.

140 The Western term "Confucianism", covering all the different schools and currents that have arisen out of the original teachings of Confucius, is in fact much broader and cruder than the particular set of thinkers designated by the Chinese "Ru Jia", which term originally meant only "the gentle ones" and only later came to mean "the school of the learned".

141 This cry was first heard at the Synod of Clermont. A fanatical crowd began to chant it when Pope Urban II, in 1095, preached a sermon calling for the military liberation of Jerusalem.

142 Confucius, Analects (With Selections from Traditional Commentaries), translated by Edward Slingerland, Hackett Publishing Company, Indianapolis/Cambridge, 2003, Chapter 1, 8, p. 3.

143 Ibid. Chapter 15, 37, p. 188.

144 Ibid. Chapter 17, 3, p. 201.

145 Ibid. Chapter 15, 15, p. 180.

146 Ibid. Chapter 9, 18, p. 92.

147 Ibid. Chapter 7, 26, p. 72 (translation altered).

148 Ibid. Chapter 7, 33, p. 75

149 Ibid. Chapter 14, 42, p. 171.

150 Ibid.

Already published in the same series:

Walther Ziegler
Adorno in 60 Minutes
ISBN 9783750460232

Walther Ziegler
Arendt in 60 Minutes
ISBN 9783752649031

Walther Ziegler
Camus in 60 Minutes
ISBN 9783741227738

Walther Ziegler
Confucius in 60 Minutes
ISBN 9783753423128

Walther Ziegler
Foucault in 60 Minutes
ISBN 978375342688

Walther Ziegler
Freud in 60 Minutes
ISBN 9783741227707

Walther Ziegler
Habermas in 60 Minutes
ISBN 9783752612370

Walther Ziegler
Hegel in 60 Minutes
ISBN 9783741227677

Walther Ziegler
Heidegger in 60 Minutes
ISBN 9783741227752

Walther Ziegler
Hobbes in 60 Minutes
ISBN 9783751968317

Walther Ziegler
Kant in 60 Minutes
ISBN 9783741226373

Walther Ziegler
Marx in 60 Minutes
ISBN 9783741227691

Walther Ziegler
Nietzsche in 60 Minutes
ISBN 9783752803822

Walther Ziegler
Rawls in 60 Minutes
ISBN 9783750424050

Walther Ziegler
Rousseau in 60 Minutes
ISBN 9783741227622

Walther Ziegler
Sartre in 60 Minutes
ISBN 9783741227653

Walther Ziegler
Smith in 60 Minutes
ISBN 9783741227721

Walther Ziegler
Platon in 60 Minutes
ISBN 9783741227615

Walther Ziegler
Popper in 60 Minutes
ISBN 9783750470897

Walther Ziegler
Schopenhauer in 60 Minutes
ISBN 9783750498853

Walther Ziegler
Wittgenstein in 60 Minutes
ISBN 9783750426955

The author:

Dr Walther Ziegler is academically trained in the fields of philosophy, history and political science. As a foreign correspondent, reporter and newsroom coordinator for the German TV station ProSieben he has produced films on every continent. His news reports have won several prizes and awards. He has also authored numerous books in the field of philosophy. His many years of experience as a journalist mean that he is able to present the complex ideas of the great philosophers in a way that is both engaging and very clear. Since 2007 he has also been active as a teacher and trainer of young TV journalists in Munich, holding the post of Academic Director at the Media Academy, a University of Applied Sciences that offers film and TV courses at its base directly on the site of the major European film production company Bavaria Film. After the huge success of the book series "Great thinkers in 60 Minutes", he works as a freelance writer and philosopher.